PETER RIDDELL is Senior Fellow at the Institute for Government and chairs the Hansard Society, having spent many years as senior political commentator on *The Times*. His many previous books include *Hug Them Close: Blair, Clinton, Bush and the 'Special Relationship'*, which won the Channel 4 Political Book of the Year Award for 2004.

In Defence of Politicians

In Defence of Politicians

(In Spite of Themselves)

Peter Riddell

First published in Great Britain in 2011 by
Biteback Publishing Ltd
Westminster Tower
3 Albert Embankment
London
SE1 7SP

ISBN 978-1-84954-037-7

10 9 8 7 6 5 4 3 2 1

A CIP catalogue record for this book is available from the British Library.

Set in Adobe Garamond Pro.
Printed and bound in Great Britain by CPI Cox & Wyman.

*For my most discerning critics and my
most loyal supporters – Avril and Emily*

CONTENTS

Preface   1

1   Introduction   11
2   Populism and excessive partisanship   25
3   Inflated expectations   41
4   Taking out the politics – and the politicians   59
5   Parliament – the stirring giant   77
6   Big bang – constitutional reform   93
7   The media – the feral beast   109
8   The verdict   135
9   What can be done   149

Bibliography   177

PREFACE

THIS BOOK IS a polemic laced with autobiography – a reflection on the nature of politics and politicians based on more than three decades of observing them. It is also a restatement of the case for representative politics, and hence for politicians, at a time when both are widely seen to be in crisis. The book has grown out of the first Parliamentary Affairs annual lecture of the same title, which I delivered in February 2010, and which was then published in a revised form in the July 2010 issue of Parliamentary Affairs. This journal is produced under the auspices of the Hansard Society, a charity which promotes representative democracy, with which I have been involved for more than a decade and a half, chairing its executive committee and council since mid-2007.

But *In Defence of Politicians* develops the argument much further than the original lecture and article. At the time of preparing the lecture, I was still chief political commentator of *The Times*. Since then, I have ceased to be a journalist after nearly forty years, including nearly thirty writing about politics, which was long enough both for me and my readers. I am still doing some freelance writing and broadcasting. But

I have taken one step back from day-to-day politics in my work as a Senior Fellow of the Institute for Government, a non-partisan charity aimed at improving the effectiveness of government. That involves looking more at procedures, systems and governance rather than immediate political events at Westminster. (Incidentally, I should stress that nothing in this book has any relevance to, or is any way affected by, the Privy Counsellor inquiry into the treatment of detainees on which I am serving.)

So my perspective on the political world has changed – from the pit to the circle. With my career as a daily journalist over, I have injected many more of my personal observations and insights from my privileged position writing about politicians at close quarters, first on the *Financial Times* up to September 1991 (including nearly three years in Washington DC), and from then until mid-2010 on *The Times*. Political journalism is a form of voyeurism: it offered me an opportunity to observe the powerful at close quarters. I was there with Margaret Thatcher and Mikhail Gorbachev in St Catherine Hall in the Kremlin, the Prime Minister at her most defiant after the Brighton bomb, and saw her interrupting a joke by Ronald Reagan (and getting away with it) at a grand dinner at the British Ambassador's residence in Washington. I saw George Bush Senior gently patronised by Deng in the Great Hall of the People in Beijing, and heard Bill Clinton deliver one of the worst political speeches I have ever heard (at the Atlanta convention in 1988) and then attempt to brazen out the Monica Lewinsky affair in early 1998 at a White House press conference, with a much more nervous Tony Blair by his side. And, along the way, I travelled the world at my employers' expense, and fell off a camel at the Pyramids.

It will be clear from my choice of title and from the subsequent chapters that, on the whole, I like politicians, though with the crucial caveat expressed in the subtitle of this book: in spite of themselves. They can be, and often are, vain, self-obsessed, narrow and blinkered. But most have a genuine commitment to public service, by which I mean helping their constituents and the public, as well as naturally themselves and their careers. So I start with a prejudice, based on close contact and knowledge, in favour of politicians as a group, and of many as individuals. In the eyes of some, as discussed in later chapters, this would class me as too much of an insider, a member of that clichéd but well understood term the Westminster village, someone who is too closely bound to its inhabitants to be able to recognise their failings. But I hope that the following chapters show that I am able to stand back and view politicians 'warts and all', as Oliver Cromwell said. Westminster, defined as the world of Parliament, can certainly be cosy like a village and inward-looking, as the expenses row and its aftermath have shown. But most MPs are well aware of how they look to outsiders. They hear complaints, often exaggerated, every day from their own constituents.

Personally, and here the confessional of the autobiography intrudes, I have instinctively sought to understand rather than instantly condemn and criticise. That has advantages for a journalist, in trying to perceive politicians' motives and viewpoints, and also what they may do next. This is not just about seeing both sides of a question, but instead mistrusting those who regard any new development in stark either/or terms. I dislike absolutes and prefer a sense of detachment and perspective. I do not regard compromise as betrayal. No aspect of life is ever 100 per cent – and those who believe it is generally come unstuck. At best, it is 80 per cent. That is one reason why the perfectionist Gordon Brown never struck a chord with voters.

Moreover, we have generally always been here before. Few policies or events are ever completely new. A ground zero mentality is both illusory and dangerous. That was what was so tiresome and vacuous about the early 'Cool Britannia' and 'young country' phase of New Labour in the mid-to-late 1990s. Few politicians or governments in democratic societies – and that qualification is obviously crucial – are either as good or bad as they are often portrayed. I am inherently suspicious of hero worship as much as the assertion that politicians are all scoundrels, and in it for themselves. This can be dismissed as being too sympathetic to politicians, but, rather, it reflects a belief that politics is both a necessary and desirable activity.

My defence of politicians is therefore not primarily a matter of personal preference. It is based on a deeper philosophical belief about how we should be governed, as I discuss in the first chapter. This involves a conscious acknowledgment of the influence of the late Bernard Crick's *In Defence of Politics*, produced nearly half a century ago in 1962. My other debts are to MPs who have championed Parliament and sought to improve it, notably recent MPs such as Dr Tony Wright, Martin Salter, Mark Fisher and David Howarth (all of whom retired at the May 2010 general election) and current ones such as Sir George Young and David Heath (at the time of writing the Leader and Deputy Leader of the Commons in the coalition respectively) and Andrew Tyrie (already making a big impact in chairing the Treasury Committee of the Commons). These MPs, and peers such as Lords Norton and Tyler, do not agree on many key issues, such as electoral reform and Lords reform, but they kept alive the flame of reform over many years. In particular, in early 2009, Tony Wright delivered the *Political Quarterly* lecture, which he had originally intended to call 'In Defence of Politicians'. But he was persuaded to abandon this title as too implausible – a caution which I have rejected. When told of the title of my lecture, many politicians, and then fellow journalists, commented that 'it needed saying', while immediately adding, in the language and tones of Sir Humphrey Appleby, you have been 'brave' and 'courageous'. However, as Tony Wright argued, 'If we want to defend politics, then we also have to defend politicians. The class of people is intrinsic to the activity.'

Depressingly few journalists have taken up this argument, preferring the easy, and populist, path of condemnation to the less popular and trickier one of understanding. However some academics, notably Andrew Gamble, Philip Cowley, Colin Hay, Gerry Stoker and Matthew Flinders, have escaped the all too frequent myopia of the world of political science and have addressed this question. Professor Flinders delivered his inaugural lecture at Sheffield University under the title of 'In Defence of Politics' just over two months after my lecture. While taking different approaches, we broadly agree on the main issues involved – and I have addressed some of the ideas in his lecture, notably on voter expectations.

I could easily have added another chapter about how many academic political scientists prove a barrier to understanding politics. To read many political science journals is to enter an enclosed and often narcissistic world of academics writing for each other – where success is marked by a mention in another academic journal. It is self-referential, as well as self-reverential, and often unreadable to anyone but a narrow group of specialists. Authors feel that they have to back up any comment, however uncontentious, by a list of citations of the work of other commentators, the disease of footnotitis. Real politicians seldom feature in their article, far less than mathematical analyses. The authors seem to feel they would be corrupted by contact with politicians. But politics is not about regression equations or neo-Marxist jargon. Some political scientists, such as the ones mentioned above and in the following pages, do try to bridge the gap with the real world of politicians and voters. But they are a minority.

The challenges to politics and politicians which form the central theme of this book are not new, but they have resurfaced in an acute form in the past two years. Recent developments potentially threaten the way that representative politics is conducted and its legitimacy, not only in Britain but also in other Western democracies. The challenge to politicians now is different both in kind and in scale. I am not seeking to defend the conduct of specific politicians: indeed their weaknesses are a major part of the problem.

The original lecture was, in part, though only in part, a response to the expenses row which engulfed British politics in the late spring of 2009. This was in itself a third wave of an anti-politician mood, the first being associated with the cash-for-questions scandal in the mid-1990s, and the second with the strong opposition to the Iraq War and the claims that Tony Blair had misled the public. However, the revelations about expenses produced an outpouring of anger and criticism of MPs generally and demands for them to be constrained and limited, and not only in their finances. So we have had not just the hurried creation of the controversial (at least with MPs) Independent Parliamentary Standards

Authority but also proposals made by all the main parties at the May 2010 general election to cut the cost of politics and give voters a greater say over what their elected representatives can do.

Much of the political and constitutional reform agenda being put forward by the coalition government is a direct result of the anguished debate over the role of MPs and Parliament ignited by the expenses row. A common theme is the attempt to show that Parliament is responding to voters' desire to control and influence their members more directly. For instance, the suggestion that MPs who are seriously in breach of ethical rules should be subject to a recall vote by their electors is intended to prevent a repetition of the Derek Conway affair in early 2008. The former Tory MP was able to remain in the Commons for another two years, despite having been found to have paid his son out of his office expenses for work which he probably did not undertake.

However, some of the proposals which emerged from the Tories' election slogan about 'cutting the cost of politics' have amounted to a muddled, and at times knee-jerk, response to the public anger over expenses. And initiatives such as reducing the number of MPs and capping the number of special advisers have produced unintended consequences and difficulties for the coalition.

Indeed, since I delivered the original lecture in February 2010, we have had the further twist of the formation of the Conservative–Liberal Democrat coalition government. The creation of the coalition has challenged many widespread preconceptions about how politics operates. Most MPs, party activists and journalists have been so accustomed to adversarial, winner-takes-all politics that they have found it hard to adjust to the bargaining and compromises inherent in multi-party politics.

That has been epitomised by that most fatuous of all complaints 'we didn't vote for that'; no, but the failure of any single party to win an overall Commons majority has meant that no one can claim the endorsement of the electorate for their platform.

Politicians have to operate in less than a winner-takes-all way. This has provoked many of the challenges which I describe in the following chapters.

This book starts with an introductory chapter setting out the main issues. It is followed by six chapters discussing the principal challenges to politicians, and then two concluding chapters discussing the implications, and outlining proposals to reinvigorate representative democracy. References to other books include the name of the author and the date of publication, with details in the bibliography. I have used the names of people as they were known at the height of their political activity, and not with any later honours or titles.

I am indebted to a very large number of politicians, journalists and friends from the past three decades. It would be invidious to single some out while excluding others. So I hope most will forgive me if I refer mainly to groups of colleagues, starting with editors and colleagues at the *Financial Times* during the 1970s and 1980s; then the varying characters who made life in *The Times* political team so such fun for nineteen years until mid-2010; the stimulating company both of my fellow council members and of the hard-working staff of the Hansard Society; and, most recently, my lively colleagues at the Institute for Government. However, I would like to mention the influence on me, and the support for me, of my two predecessors in chairing Hansard (David Butler and the late, and much missed, Richard Holme), as well as the many thought-provoking conversations over the decades with my good friends Andrew Adonis (to whom I am very grateful for reading a draft of this book), Helene Hayman, Peter Hennessy, Roger Liddle, James Naughtie and Andrew Tyrie. I always gain fresh insights from talking to them. On the publishing side, I am, as always, grateful to Sean Magee, my ever-patient editor in various guises over nearly thirty years, and to Iain Dale, the moving spirit behind Biteback who has done so much to stimulate public debate about politics in his various publishing and other activities.

Finally, I am indebted, as always, to my family, my wife Avril and my now teenage daughter Emily for their support and love – indulging my strange obsession with politics (only rivalled by cricket) and tolerating, most of the time, the associated accumulation of books and paper.

Peter Riddell
February 2011

CHAPTER ONE

INTRODUCTION

POLITICIANS HAVE NEVER been popular. Their motives and behaviour have always been questioned. They have been seen as devious, factional and self-interested, pursuing sectional rather than national interests. Shakespeare referred to 'scurvy politicians' in *King Lear*. We all know Henry Carey's words from 300 years ago in the national anthem: 'Confound their politics, Frustrate their knavish tricks.' In a non-democratic age, this reflected a particular, royal and court view of the national interest above the intrigues of aristocratic factions. In the following century, Robert Cecil, the future late-Victorian Prime Minister, and, admittedly, never an optimist about the political scene, in 1860 complained about the 'incompetence and laziness of MPs'. There was never a golden age and it is possible to find quotations in almost any decade deploring the low standing of politicians. They are seen as corrupt and selfish as well as figures of fun: just look at the wonderful tradition of caricature and satire from Swift and Hogarth, via Gillray and

Rowlandson, up to the puppets of *Spitting Image* in the 1980s and the biting political cartoons of Peter Brookes and Steve Bell. But politicians have not just been seen as ridiculous. They have also, increasingly, been regarded as ineffective.

Criticism of the political class, and Parliament, has, if anything, intensified since the creation of a mass electorate after the extension of the franchise in 1918. During the 1920s, MPs were seen as ineffective and of low quality, unequal to the task of controlling the big expansion of the state bureaucracy as central government took on more economic and social responsibilities.

This led during the 1930s to demands from many on the left for an even stronger executive to tackle the problem of mass unemployment. Elected politicians in Parliament should be relegated to a secondary, almost rubber-stamp, role approving enabling legislation which would confer wide-ranging general powers on ministers and civil servants. Even the most successful of democratic politicians recognise their isolation. Take a saying from the other side of the Atlantic:

> Politicians are a set of men who have interests aside from the interests of the people, and who are, taken as a mass, at least one long step removed from honest men. I say this with the greatest freedom because, being a politician myself, none can regard it as personal.

The speaker was a young Illinois lawyer politician, no not Barack Obama, but that master politician, Abraham Lincoln, in 1837.

Lincoln summed up the paradox of the politician as someone seen as apart from the mass of the people, even though, in a democratic age, a politician is dependent for success on the votes of those same people. We love criticising politicians but we cannot do without them. Politicians as a class are integral to representative politics. You cannot have one without the other. It is essential also to throw political parties into the mix: they provide cohesion and direction, despite the views of some who now favour direct democracy without politicians and parties in their current form. Politics is inherently a rough and messy business, and I have no wish to pretend otherwise.

Two apparently contradictory trends are operating, both working against the current generation of politicians. The first, and most widespread, is to denigrate all politicians as a class. This involves an implicit, and often explicit, statement of superiority by the critics. The People, often with a capital P, know best and they are invariably duped by wrong-headed and self-serving politicians. Second, contemporary politicians are seen as inferior to more enlightened, and purer, ones in the past. They are seen as pygmies compared with the alleged giants from a golden age. Something has happened inbetween to produce a decline in standards and conduct.

Peter Oborne brought these strands together in a fierce attack on the new generation of politicians in his 2007 book, *The Triumph of the Political Class*. Oborne argued that they form the new ruling elite of Britain, a group characterised by its professional attitude to politics rather than old-fashioned ideology, and which has made party political differences non-existent in its pursuit of power and patronage. The new political class is not only set apart from the rest of society, with its own manners, morality and habits, but is also actively hostile to ordinary people and common modes of life in defending its special privileges, regulations and pay. 'British politicians have sought to govern in a novel way, obliterating the organisations and methods of representative democracy and instead using the press and broadcast media as the key method of communication between ruler and ruled.' You can, however, also argue the reverse case that politicians are too supine towards the pretensions of the press and broadcasters.

Oborne is an acute journalist and a formidable polemicist, but often goes 10 to 20 per cent too far in his sweeping judgements. He tends to claim that a government or a politician is the 'most corrupt ever', or that an event spells 'doom' or 'triumph'. In reality, politics is more shaded and nuanced. But his view of a self-contained, and out of touch, political class is widely shared as part of the populist attack I discuss in the next chapter.

A variant of this argument is that politicians start off well but are then corrupted after being elected or once they accept ministerial office. But, just as hero worship inevitably leads to disappointment and disillusion, so pretending politicians are better than they are, or ever can be, is a fatuous exercise. So I am careful to talk about politicians, not statesmen, a pompous term liked by golden ageists and those who mistrust the political process and who falsely try to raise leaders out of the rough and tumble of the daily political battle.

Some of the most respected, and successful, past leaders – Abraham Lincoln, Franklin Roosevelt, Winston Churchill, Margaret Thatcher – were instinctive politicians to their fingertips. To pretend otherwise, to canonise them, is to do them a profound disservice: retrospective hagiography invariably distorts their real contributions. The way that the names of Ronald Reagan and Margaret Thatcher are still regularly invoked on the right in the hope of scoring points in current debates – they would not have done this or that – is both depressing and misleading. They were both formidable leaders during the 1980s in changing the terms of the political debate, and had many achievements to their credit. But, like all politicians, they were of their times, and had well-known strengths and weaknesses. Above all, they were mortal. Reagan was fortunate in the post-FDR constitutional amendment limiting a US President to just two terms, or eight years.

Thatcher tempted the fates and was forced out in November 1990 by her own Cabinet and MPs after eleven and a half years. The first signs of hubris came more than three and a half years earlier in spring 1987 while returning from a highly successful pre-election trip to the Soviet Union to meet, and argue with, Mikhail Gorbachev. This success was reinforced by the contrasting embarrassment of Neil Kinnock's brief visit to the White House just a few days earlier (a failure partly orchestrated by Charles Powell, her foreign policy adviser, with Reagan's own staff). Talking to reporters, including me, crammed in the back of the RAF VC10 returning to London, Thatcher made her first reference to 'going on and on'. Standing next to me, Bernard Ingham, her devoted press secretary, said to me, only half complaining: 'Now, I will never be able to retire.' He could, and did, but it would have been better for her if she had not gone on for so long.

The attempt by Thatcher's more fervent supporters, in the No Turning Back group and elsewhere, to maintain the myth of betrayal ignored how dangerously out of touch she had become, as well as alienated from former close allies such as Nigel Lawson and Geoffrey Howe. By failing to treat her as a mortal politician, these Thatcherite ultras tarnished her own reputation and fatally undermined the government of her successor, John Major.

Politicians should not aspire to be saints, or treated by their followers as saints – that is the way to disaster. They are mortal and flawed. Their role is not to create an ideal society – that illusion can be left to fanatics whether fascist or communist – but, rather, to help reconcile different interests in a peaceful way.

Politics recognises, even celebrates, the clash of views and of groups, but within a framework of broadly agreed rules defined by regular elections within a representative democracy, underpinned by the rule of law. This requires mutual respect, and mutual constraints, between not just political leaders and their MPs but also their members and supporters. All have to accept the legitimacy of an election result. The other side may be wrong, but it has every right to its opinions and to implement its policies if it has won a free election. Equally, the winning side should accept constraints: the need for proper scrutiny of its proposals and the right of the opposition, and of minority and outside groups, to express their opinions.

Bernard Crick's *In Defence of Politics* set out many challenges to politics, and therefore politicians: from authoritarians and ideologues, from what he vividly called the 'saints' or 'student politicians' who believe that the cause of the moment is all that matters (like many single-issue pressure groups), from technocrats and mandarins who see themselves as superior to politics and from those who condemn any deviation from their ramrod principles as betrayal. The essence of politics is recognising imperfection; we can do better but cannot create a perfect society. All these challenges set out by Crick remain, but there are many newer ones, created both by the collapse of deference towards an established political class (on the whole a healthy development except where it slips into destructive cynicism) and by technological developments such as the growth of the internet which have opened up access to political debate (again healthy in itself but subject to abuse). The end of deference has fuelled calls for increased transparency and created a more uninhibited, and critical, attitude towards politicians. That has been reflected in lower levels of trust in politicians, as well as in other public figures and institutions. There is an intriguing question about which is symptom and which cause.

Politicians are therefore on the defensive, and prickly, as reflected in the widespread anger of MPs about the much tighter rules imposed by IPSA. They feel misunderstood and misjudged. Despite their many failings, they have a strong case. By and large, most politicians are not in public life just for themselves, or to become better off. Of course, ego and vanity play a large part – often a large part – as they do in any occupation involving public performance. Many journalists are hardly lacking in ego and vanity, even more so than many leading politicians since media stars are mostly in a less vulnerable position. But there is also a large measure of public service, not least because of their direct contacts with constituents, which are more regular than in the past.

During the early 1960s I lived in Streatham whose MP was Duncan Sandys, a son-in-law of Winston Churchill, who was mainly seen at election time speaking from a loud-hailer being driven up and down Streatham High Road. His response to criticism of his infrequent appearances was that he had been elected to represent 'Streatham in Westminster, not Westminster in Streatham' – even though the two are less than half an hour apart by car, bus or train. Similarly, just after arriving at Westminster as a political journalist in 1981, I heard Sir

Patrick Wall, a genuine Tory knight of the shires, not just an ersatz one from the suburbs, talk about his annual visit around his constituency. The clumsy phrasing of his remark produced subdued guffaws among the few MPs present in the Commons chamber. Most MPs knew that what Sir Patrick meant was his annual September visit around his geographically large rural seat with many small villages.

However, this was still the time when urban Labour MPs for supposedly safe seats as well as Tory squires thought they could safely neglect their constituencies, with only occasional visits and, in a few cases, not bother replying to correspondence from their voters. That complacency was ended by a combination of Labour's acceptance in the early 1980s of mandatory re-selection of MPs, the growing challenge from Liberal, then Liberal Democrat, candidates, and the increasing demands from constituents who felt they had a right to service from their MPs.

Most MPs work hard at Westminster and their constituencies for little thanks. Personal financial reward usually comes low down their priorities and the abuse of lax expenses rules was in many, though not all, cases a response to the holding down of MPs' pay. However, this view is not widely shared outside the Palace of Westminster. Opinion poll after opinion poll has confirmed the low standing of politicians, while turnout fell sharply in the 2001 general election, and has only partially recovered since then. Moreover, participation in political parties is low by comparison with the immediate post-war period. A Populus poll for *The Times* in February 2010 showed that the political system as a whole came bottom in a ranking of public satisfaction with various aspects of British life. The NHS was top. Nearly three-quarters of voters think politics is broken in

Britain, while almost a half believed their local constituency MP abused the system of parliamentary expenses and allowances.

It is scant comfort that the post-expenses reaction does not represent a sudden decline in the public's view of politicians. Their standing has been pretty low for some time, as has been underlined by the annual Audit of Political Engagement from the Hansard Society, based on interviews by Ipsos MORI. This is particularly valuable since each year the survey asks similar questions about voters' knowledge, attitudes and levels of political activity. The expenses scandal has not resulted in a fundamental change in the public's views about MPs largely because voters were pretty sceptical anyway. So, while the 2010 Audit showed that trust in politicians did not collapse, it was already at a low level with just 26 per cent saying they trusted politicians 'a great deal' or 'a fair amount', down just one point on the first Audit report in 2004. However, public satisfaction with how Parliament works has dropped sharply: from 36 per cent in 2004 to 33 per cent in the 2010 Audit, in the immediate aftermath of the expenses row, and down to a low of just 27 per cent in the 2011 version. Around 40 per cent of people continue to believe that the UK Parliament 'holds government to account', but fewer voters now agree that Parliament is 'working for you and me' (30 per cent in the latest Audit, down from 38 per cent a year earlier). Therefore, for the first time, more people disagree (39 per cent) than agree (30 per cent) that Parliament is 'working for you and me'.

The 2011 Audit (the eighth in the series, based on interviews in December 2010) shows, however, that the proportion of people claiming to know at least 'a fair amount' about Parliament has risen to 44 per cent, compared with 33 per cent seven years ago. This, of course, followed a general election year and the formation of the coalition. However, fewer than two-fifths could correctly name their local MP, possibly reflecting the high turnover of MPs at the May election.

Ambiguity also exists over the role of MPs. Most voters believe that MPs put their own interests first, while roughly a half think they should be concentrating on their constituents' interests. MPs complain, often accurately, that they cannot win. Their voters complain if they are not in their constituency, while they are attacked in the media for taking long holidays whenever Parliament goes into recess – though the Commons and Lords sit for longer than most other legislatures. MPs are much more assiduous in their constituency work than their predecessors half a century ago. Indeed, one worry is that they have become too constituency-oriented, at the expense of their work at Westminster.

There is also a marked contrast in the public's view of how most MPs spend their time, and how they should spend their time. For instance, according to the 2010 version of the Audit, 50 per cent of those interviewed believed that most MPs spend their time furthering their personal and career interests, while just 3 per cent thought they should be doing so. As damagingly, 46 per cent thought MPs should be spending their time representing the views of local people in the House of Commons, while just 10 per cent believed they were doing so. In reality, whatever else you feel about the current generation of politicians, they are much more active in representing the views of local people than their predecessors ever were. But, again, the perception gap is critical.

Similar trends are shown by the annual survey of British Social Attitudes. According to the twenty-seventh report in December 2010, 40 per cent said they 'almost never trust' governments to put the national interest first. This is a six-point rise above the previous all-time high of 34 per cent in 2006 – which was in the aftermath of the recriminations following the Iraq War – and around four times as high as the levels in the late 1980s (11 per cent in 1987). There is little sign that the expenses scandal has reduced peoples' interest in politics. A third of those questioned said they have 'a great deal', or 'quite a lot', of interest in politics, much the same as over the period since the early 1990s.

The causes for the decline in trust in politicians, and, even more, possible ways of rebuilding it, are not straightforward, as I will discuss in more detail in later chapters. Some reforms aimed at restoring trust, such as greater transparency and accountability, can have unintended and counter-productive effects. After all, details of MPs' expenses only became known because of a post-1997 reform initiative, Freedom of Information legislation, and the disclosures have made the public more suspicious. That is not an argument about FOI legislation or other reforms, but, rather, a recognition that focusing on trust in politicians may be missing some of the main questions about the perceived effectiveness of MPs.

Following the expenses scandal, there has been a sharp change in public attitudes about the impact of Parliament on peoples' lives. According to the 2011 Audit, just 30 per cent say Parliament is one of the top three institutions that make an impact on their lives. The real worry for MPs is that many voters see them as less relevant. But turnout increased in the 2010 election. Moreover, voters still look to politicians to sort out their problems. For all the disparagement of politicians which I set out in the coming chapters, there has been no crisis of the state. Taxes are still paid; laws are generally obeyed.

Admittedly, the public's longstanding lack of trust in politicians is hardly unique among Western democracies. According to the European Social Survey, over one in ten Europeans have no trust in politicians and a half report low levels of trust. But the Eurobarometer survey of opinion across the EU has consistently found that the British are less trustful of a range of institutions – government, Parliament, the political parties, the EU and the Commission – than their counterparts in the rest of Europe.

Nonetheless, as Colin Hay argued (2007), there have been long-standing trends towards political disengagement in most Western democracies: a long-term decline in turnout levels at elections since the 1960s, with some acceleration since the 1990s; growing voter cynicism, especially among younger and better educated voters; significant long-term declines in levels of political trust; and high levels of contempt for politicians and political institutions.

However, the expenses scandal in spring 2009 did produce a crisis of self-awareness among politicians. Many MPs may have thought that most of the criticisms were unfair but they could not ignore them. One early Friday afternoon in late spring 2009, I bumped into one London MP whom I knew by name, but not well, in the ticket hall of Westminster underground station. It was one of those now rare Fridays when the Commons had been sitting. He was about to head home to his constituency. But he said to me, almost despairingly, 'I can't face it, I don't want to go.' And this from an MP who had a perfectly defensible, and above board, record on expenses, not least because as a London member he could not claim the allowance for additional housing costs which caused much of the controversy. But he was afraid of the ill-informed insults which he would receive on the street from his constituents. That was a vivid illustration of the low standing of members.

The debate about politicians goes much further than their personal conduct. It is really about what type of democracy we want. Most of the challenges which I discuss in the following chapters turn on a mistrust of politicians, and a reluctance to cede power and responsibility to them. As I make clear later in the book, I believe the balance has to shift. The elitist assumptions dating back to a pre-democratic age that voters should have no role between elections are wrong and unsustainable. There is scope for more direct voter control over decisions affecting their lives whether through greater voice – via more elections or referendums – or greater choice – via greater diversity of provision of services. But there are limits to direct participation. We still need representatives to mediate and reconcile our differing interests. Citizens' juries and other deliberative mechanisms for considering policy options may help to clarify choices. While the people participating may emerge better informed and wiser, they can only represent themselves. They cannot, and should not, speak for the rest of us. There is still no substitute for elected politicians balancing out competing claims on taxation and public expenditure, or taking often difficult decisions in foreign, defence and counter-terrorism policy. A representative system, and the cohesion provided by political parties, provide authority and direction which cannot be achieved in a system of direct democracy. Politicians are needed to make and implement hard choices. But their ability to perform these roles has been undermined not only by their own failures but also by the new challenges which are set out in the following chapters.

CHAPTER TWO

POPULISM AND EXCESSIVE PARTISANSHIP

THE MOST FREQUENT charge against politicians is that they are self-serving scoundrels. They are in it for themselves and to hell with the lot of them. That view has a long history in British politics. As noted earlier, politicians have been the frequent butt of satirists and cartoonists. But the populist revolt has taken a new, and uglier, turn recently, and is closely allied to excessive partisanship.

Politicians have given plenty of ammunition to their critics in the last few years – hence the 'in spite of themselves' subtitle of this book. There was the cash for questions affair in the mid-1990s which led to a big tightening in regulation on lobbying by MPs and outside interests. The term 'sleaze' then entered the political lexicon, to be used about any MP thought, however flimsily, to be guilty of improper conduct – just as 'spin' began to be used a few years later about any attempt by the Blair government to influence the media. Yet largely unknown to the media as well as the public, a further scandal was brewing in the abuse of MPs' expenses. The daily series of revelations about these expenses in the *Daily Telegraph* in the spring of 2009 has been more damaging than anything else to the popular standing of Parliament, leading to the departure from the Commons of a number of prominent MPs and criminal convictions, and prison, for a handful. The House of Lords has not been immune either, for all its liking to claim superiority to the Commons: in 2009, following a sting operation by the *Sunday Times*, two Labour peers were suspended – the first exercise of such powers in more than 350 years – for expressing a willingness to amend legislation for money. In 2010, more peers were suspended, for a longer period, for falsely claiming money for second homes, Lord Taylor of Warwick was convicted of false accounting and a further two were fortunate not to face criminal charges.

I discuss in later chapters the impact of the expenses scandal on voter expectations about MPs and on Parliament itself. Much of the criticism was justified, but it went too far. However outrageous – and in some cases criminal – the conduct of some MPs was, and however distasteful the sense of entitlement which many more MPs claimed, our political class remains pretty clean by international standards. Indeed, foreign commentators were bemused by the small scale and bizarre character of the expense claims in dispute.

There were three broad categories of MPs: first, the small number who have broken the law (and have received, or face, prison sentences for making false claims); second, a larger group of perhaps three or four dozen MPs who clearly abused the spirit, if not the letter, of the previous system by their greed and lack of moral judgement (most of whom left the Commons before the 2010 general election); and, third, the majority of MPs whose repayments were more the result of administrative incompetence than any personal abuses (via problems of the timing of mortgage payments and the like). However, too many MPs were complicit in a lax system. Public perceptions of MPs' conduct were not helped by the flawed rough justice of Sir Thomas Legg's inquiry into members' expenses, naming a large number of MPs who were asked to repay money. So trying to defend, or at least explain, the conduct of the majority of MPs in the third group has been next to impossible. A majority of MPs behaved properly, or made, at most, inadvertent mistakes. Tony Blair – improbably given his lack of interest in most of his fellow MPs – has made the most robust defence in his memoirs (2010):

> the savaging of MPs as basically a bunch of wasters and fraudsters was unjust and deeply damaging. As ever with such an outpouring of outrage, the innocent or the mildly stupid have been executed along with those who really did cross the line. It is a real shame that no one stuck up for the MPs. Instead, everyone competed in condemnation of them.

Moreover, MPs did not help their own defence, not only by their acquiescence in a flawed system (as discussed in a later chapter) but also by their response to the publication of the charges in spring 2009. The world of Westminster can be deeply unattractive to outsiders – complacent, arrogant and insensitive. Many senior MPs circled the wagons and refused to recognise the legitimacy of the demands for disclosure and reform. Even after all the traumas of the past two years, and even after the arrival of so many new MPs at the 2010 general election (36 per cent, a few percentage points less than in 1997), too many members have been resistant to change. This has been shown not just in the controversy over the Independent Parliamentary Standards Authority but also over procedural reforms to make Parliament more responsive. MPs are often too timid in defending themselves and their role. The House of Lords has also been slow to appreciate the need to be more accountable publicly, despite prodding by the Lord Speaker and some shrewder peers. Part of the reason may be that, while MPs are, in general, forced to face public views by contact with their constituents, peers have no constituents. Too many peers just talk among themselves, reinforcing a sense of injured self-righteousness. The culture of Westminster is still too inward-looking and contemptuous towards outsiders. Admittedly, progress has been made by the Commons and Lords as institutions – notably by the current Mr Speaker and the Lord Speaker – in what is inelegantly called 'parliamentary outreach', explaining what happens at Westminster to schools and the public. And many MPs and peers do their bit. But, too often, the response to scandals such as the expenses disclosures or complaints over the conduct of MPs and peers has been prickly and defensive, reinforcing the public anger and the populist mood.

It is hard to put the recent controversies into perspective. For instance, there has been practically none of the corruption over the award of contracts involving politicians often seen in the United States and many European countries. Contracts and new spending projects are often awarded to marginal constituencies ahead of general elections, a British version of American pork barrel politics. But there is no personal financial benefit to politicians. Moreover, most MPs are not required to raise large sums of money personally, thanks to controls on spending at a constituency level dating back to the late nineteenth century. Before then, financial corruption was rife in election campaigns. The need to raise money has anyway been limited both by controls on total spending and by the ban on television and radio advertisements by parties. These ensure that the total cost of a British general election campaign can be less than is spent by candidates in a big state's elections. For instance, Meg Whitman, the losing Republican candidate for Governor of California in November 2010, spent a record $173 million, while Jerry Brown, the Democrat victor, spent $44 million. These sums were exceptional, but candidates for the Senate in large states routinely spend as much as the maximum a British party is allowed to spend in a general election. And in Britain the main fundraising is done by parties, not by individual politicians.

The main scandals in Britain have been over allegations that financial donations, or, before the 2005 election, loans, have been made to political parties by wealthy individuals in the hope/expectation of receiving an honour. The correlation between donations and awards of knighthoods and peerages has been more than coincidental – and it has unquestionably damaged the standing of politicians. More of that link is now known thanks to the legislation setting up the Electoral Commission and requiring full disclosure, while the ability to 'purchase' a peerage has become harder by the much tougher policing by the House of Lords Appointments Commission. Of course, the 'loans for peerages' allegations which cast a shadow over the end of the Blair premiership damaged politicians, even though no criminal charges were made.

The overall impact of these various scandals has been seen not only in the low standing of politicians in the poll (existing well before the expenses scandal) but also in a mood of popular contempt for politicians generally. Any attempt by a senior MP to draw the distinctions which I have made was scornfully dismissed on TV programmes with audiences like *Question Time*. The greatest applause was invariably for attacks on politicians from one of the 'celebrity panellists' – who seem to be chosen for knowing nothing about politics.

The mood of the time has been summed up in the success of Heather Brooke, the freedom of information campaigner who helped – along with some redoubtable and persistent journalists – to secure the publication of MPs' expenses. This was before the key computer disk with all the details was leaked, and then published by the *Daily Telegraph*. This has been one of Brooke's many campaigns against an obstructive and secretive state. Her record against the obduracy of local councils, against distorted statistics and secret justice is impressive. And many of her opponents – from elusive bureaucrats to the hapless Commons Speaker Michael Martin and other senior MPs who resisted disclosure of expenses – are easy to cast as villains. Martin failed as Speaker because he primarily thought of himself as a shop steward on behalf of MPs and failed to appreciate the need for leadership to clean up the mess and help restore the standing of the Commons. In this he was certainly not alone, and other MPs and Commons officials share the blame. Like many single-issue campaigners, Brooke's virtues and vices are inextricably linked. Their determination and tunnel vision often make them self-righteous, obsessive and lacking proportion. So her justified campaign against secrecy over MPs' expenses has often been made to appear a monochrome 'goodies versus baddies' struggle in which the whole political class is condemned. In her book *The Silent State* (2010), she offers a blanket denunciation of the political class. She fails to acknowledge that it was these very politicians, and, in particular, the Labour government, that introduced the very Freedom of Information legislation she has used so assiduously. However, Tony Blair later repented of the Freedom of Information Act as being 'utterly undermining of sensible government' in a revealing passage of his autobiography (2010). Brooke also shows little appreciation of the largely unheralded work which MPs do on behalf of their constituents or in Commons committees.

Brooke is interesting – not just for her campaigns but because she, like many populists, is at heart an anti-government libertarian, a Jeffersonian in a Hobbesian world. She believes in largely self-governing communities with active citizens like herself, in which the state and politicians are largely redundant. But not everyone is like her, active and committed to asserting their rights. Most of us are not, and even if we were, we would still need some means of balancing and reconciling different opinions and interests. This is what politics is about. But in her book Brooke almost completely ignores the role of the representative, whether a local councillor or MP, in taking up individual grievances against the state bureaucracies she condemns.

This anti-politician populist mood has been fuelled by much of the media and, particularly, by the internet and social media sites. If you think the tabloid newspapers have been increasingly strident in their attacks on privileged politicians, just look at some of the main political websites. In themselves, sites such as ConservativeHome, the most successful of the politically aligned ones, provide a welcome broadening of political discussion and debate, making up for the reduction in the range of coverage in most conventional newspapers. But many of the comments attached even to largely sensible posts are hate-filled rants, invariably anonymous since their cowardly authors are unwilling to declare their identities. The leading sites do filter out personally offensive anonymous posts, but others are less assiduous in the time-consuming task of moderating comments. Despite exclusion of the most defamatory comments, many are still offensive and contemptuous of anyone with whom they disagree, which means most politicians who are invariably regarded as venal and useless. Sneering contempt is expressed for anyone else's motives or points of view. There is a 'them and us' mentality in which the legitimacy of opponents is questioned in childish terms. There is seldom even the slightest hint of any understanding of the complexities of government, or that politicians are trying their best, however mistaken they may be. Too often the comments reek of paranoia and reflect the inadequacy of the unfulfilled who get their satisfaction, such as it is, by posting such vituperative anonymous attacks. Gordon Brown was frequently denigrated in the most vitriolic, personally offensive, terms – in part because he had allegedly been 'unelected', ignoring that in a parliamentary system his succession to Tony Blair in June 2007 had been constitutionally legitimate.

Many of the worst excesses are shown by the comments on the Guido Fawkes site – more than three-fifths of which were judged to be negative, according to an academic review by John Robertson and Elizabeth McLaughlin (2011). This compares with an average of 20 per cent on a range of newspaper and independent sites. Guido Fawkes is the pseudonym for a financial trader called Paul Staines, whose whole approach is muckraking and anti-establishment. He has some important scoops to his credit, beating what he derides as the 'dead tree' mainstream press. He can also be original and refreshingly contrary to the conventional wisdom in some of his analysis and commentary. But his site encourages a scurrilous cynicism about politicians and does not recognise any line between their public and private lives. Some of the comments posted on the site are extremely offensive and vulgar in personal terms not only about leading politicians but also about fellow bloggers, not rising above the level of graffiti.

Allied to this anti-politician populism is excessive partisanship. That does not mean no partisanship. I am inherently suspicious of people who talk about being above politics or party. That is frequently an excuse for self-righteous dogmatism or self-interest. Appeals to bipartisanship can often amount to humbug. Of course, personal and national tragedies such as terrorist acts or natural disasters should be handled with restraint rather than be used for point scoring. But too often attempts at self-conscious bipartisanship can result in a suspension of proper scrutiny and accountability. Occasions when the House of Commons unites and are said to be at its best can be the reverse, exercises in pious platitudes, necessary perhaps to handle immediate grief, but, rightly, unsustainable. Moreover, some of the worst legislation in recent decades has been speedily passed by Parliament with bipartisan support – such as the Dangerous Dogs Act, which produced apparently arbitrary and largely unenforceable distinctions between breeds of dog, and the creation of the Child Support Agency, with its cumbersome and costly administration.

However, politicians who want to make a lasting mark need to ensure that their policies are, in time, accepted by their opponents. This is partly because many major reforms take years to implement and work through the system. It is no good a minister taking a highly partisan approach to, say, a major infrastructure project like high-speed rail or civil nuclear power, or to pension reform, if the opposition party is going to scrap it. So wise, and successful, ministers do try to engage their opposition shadows, in private if not always in public, in the hope of obtaining their acquiescence and preferably support. Sometimes this is also shrewd electoral politics.

An effective democracy requires the expression of different views and parties to articulate them. Parties, like football teams, tend to be tribal, exaggerating differences. But just as obscene chants and football hooliganism are the unacceptable side of what is often ludicrously called the 'beautiful game', so strident and intemperate attacks on opponents are the unacceptable face of representative democracy. If politics is essentially a question of balance, of compromise and reconciliation, then it means accepting that the other side has a legitimate right to be heard and, if it wins enough votes, to form a government. Your opponents may be wrong-headed and have pursued the wrong policies, which is why you are not in their party. They not only have a right to exist, but their existence is central to representative democracy. The basic test of any democratic system is the peaceful shift of power from one party to another.

These assumptions on balance are undermined by excessive partisanship. The integrity of politicians, and the legitimacy of the transfer of power after elections, is now being challenged even in supposedly advanced democracies. Such protests may still come from a minority, but they exist – and their voice has been amplified by the existence of the internet. Apart from the tumultuous period before 1914, the conventions of parliamentary politics have exercised a constraint on verbal excesses. But now activists and partisans on the internet are less constrained, and more willing to challenge the legitimacy of the 'swing of the pendulum'. That is not just the result of the broadening of the media debate through the internet, but may also reflect the frustrations which built up during two long periods of one party rule – from 1979 until 1997 under the Conservatives, and then until 2010 under Labour.

Similar extreme partisanship has been expressed since the creation of the Conservative–Liberal Democrat coalition in May 2010. Complaints have been heard that the coalition lacks a mandate and no one voted for its policies. They have come not just from the left and Labour, but also, more revealingly, from disaffected members of the two coalition parties. The Conservative right, both inside and outside the Commons, and the Liberal Democrat left both complain that too many concessions are being made to the other side. But these arguments from activists miss the point. We have a coalition because no single party won a majority of seats in the Commons. In these circumstances, it is the duty of politicians and the main parties to reach compromises so that government can carry on. The critics do not seem to have considered that the alternative would not have been the enactment of their proposals, but, rather, an ineffective minority administration trying, and failing, to enact measures which do not have the support of a majority of MPs, let alone voters.

The position is much worse in the United States. A substantial minority on the populist right, including among Republican identifiers, have questioned the legitimacy of Barack Obama's position as President, despite his success in winning the highest percentage of the popular vote for two decades. The 'birther' movement has claimed that Barack Obama is not qualified to be President in view of flimsily based allegations that he was not born in the USA. (This is often tied in with suggestions that in view of his second name Hussein, he is a secret Muslim, despite his long-established Christian commitment and involvement.) The passion, and unreason, behind such allegations is a denial of the conventions which are essential to the working of representative democracy. Republican congressmen have called the president 'an enemy of humanity', questioning his patriotism. It is commonplace on the populist right to describe him as a socialist – a weird charge to anyone remotely familiar with social democracy, let alone democratic socialism. Even among more mainstream Republicans, as well as House Democrats, there has been a 'slash-and-burn' approach of extreme partisanship. Indeed, it was only after the Democrats suffered a drubbing in the November 2010 mid-term congressional elections, losing control of the House of Representatives and seeing their majority cut in the Senate, that compromises were reached. During the lame duck session of Congress before the Republicans took control of the House in January 2011, important legislation was enacted on taxation and ratifying a treaty on strategic arms limitation. This reflected greater tactical flexibility by President Obama in working with Congress.

The classic example of excessive partisanship – as well as of populism – is the Tea Party Movement which came into existence in the USA following President Obama's inauguration. Its roots are complicated but the key link between its diverse elements is dislike of big government, including the Federal Reserve. The impetus came from the long wrangle over the Obama administration's healthcare legislation which was presented as not only an extension of the state's power (an alleged step towards socialised medicine, as in Britain), but also as a limitation on patients' choice. Many of the charges were greatly distorted since much of American medical care, for the elderly and the poor, is already heavily subsidised by the taxpayers. The resentment of the state took many forms but was undoubtedly fuelled by the combination of the deep recession with its associated rise in unemployment and resentment at Washington's bailout of the big investment banks. As the name implies, the movement was inspired by the Boston Tea Party protest against taxes imposed by the London government on the American colonists. This has been associated with a literal-minded interpretation of the American Constitution, which was drafted in 1787. So only actions specifically authorised by the Constitution should become law. This was not only seen as ruling out healthcare legislation but, taken literally, it would also put a question mark against funding for the American airforce since the Wright brothers' first flight came more than a century after the approval of the Constitution.

The various Tea Party groups have been united in wanting to cut back the size of government, by eliminating or slashing federal spending programmes. Tax increases of any kind were vigorously opposed. The Tea Party has also been fervently patriotic, backing strong action against suspected terrorists and favouring a robust defence posture. It has also vigorously opposed gun controls and defended the right to bear arms as set out in the second amendment to the Constitution. As Kate Zernike (2010) discusses in her revealing book about Tea Party activists, there have also been many contradictions in its positions. Tea Party supporters may oppose big government, but woe betide any politician who threatens their social security payments (retirement pensions) or Medicare (health support). As often, voters dislike all government programmes apart from those which benefit them.

The underlying anti-politician populism meant that their attacks encompassed some moderate Republicans as well as Democrats. Tea Party candidates ousted some sitting and establishment Republicans in party primaries. However, the winners of these primaries did not do so well in the November elections for the Senate – though they did much better in the House. But the main impact of the Tea Party movement has been to energise Republican activists and the right after the defeats of 2006 and 2008 and has rallied them behind the counter-attacks led by Sarah Palin, the former Governor of Alaska and Republican vice-presidential candidate. The main enemy has been seen as President Obama who is described as a dictator, a liar and unpatriotic. These charges of being un-American and illegitimate threaten the whole basis of representative democracy.

The Tea Party movement has also become associated with some of the nuttier, and even violent, fringes of the American right where dislike of big government shifts into paranoia, xenophobia and even hints of violence. This is not new. There is a long tradition of anti-government populism going back to the anti-immigrant nativist groups of the nineteenth century. Many of the charges which President Obama has faced were also made against Franklin Roosevelt in the 1930s (apart from those associated with the former's birth and, implicitly, his race). Father Coughlin, the radio ranter of the 1930s, has his successors in Rush Limbaugh and Glenn Beck, the Fox television presenter, who has, for example, accused George Soros, the financier, of being a 'puppet-master' intent on the overthrow of the American government.

These tensions surfaced in January 2011 in the aftermath of the attempted assassination of congresswoman Gabrielle Giffords and the killing of six other people, including a Federal judge, in Tuscon, Arizona. It is a gross over-simplification to link the alleged assailant with the vitriolic and increasingly partisan tone of American political debate. And he had no apparent connection with Tea Party groups. Nor was there evidence that he was inspired by what he had heard or seen in the media. There is a long history, especially in the United States, of disturbed people with access to firearms resorting to attacks on public figures, or right-wing extremists attacking the state, as in the bombing of the Oklahoma City Federal Building which killed 168 people. However, it is indicative of the polarised mood that the Arizona shootings prompted a debate about whether political language had got out of hand. The violent imagery – even pictures featuring guns – has unquestionably heightened the emotional level of debate on talk shows, on blogs and on Twitter, which encourages extremism.

Typically, perhaps, the extremists on both right and left blamed the other for exploiting the Arizona tragedy. But there was, at least, a pause across most of the political and media worlds for restraint and reflection – that democracy is polluted and threatened by casting doubt on the legitimacy of your opponents.

In Britain, politics has not yet become so extreme or polarised as in the USA. However, the combination of long periods of a single party in power, well-publicised abuses by some MPs and a populist reaction assisted by the internet and bloggers has fuelled an anti-politician rhetoric which questions the legitimacy of political opponents. At its most idiotic, this has been seen in the fact that far-left protesters against spending cuts and increases in tuition fees absurdly compare their attempt to throw out the elected government here with the mass demonstrations against authoritarian regimes in the Arab world. But there has been a wider populist and excessively partisan tone to political debate – both in the media and among party activists – which undermines politicians and representative democracy.

CHAPTER THREE

INFLATED EXPECTATIONS

ONE OF THE most serious threats to politicians comes from false and exaggerated expectations. Many voters have unrealistic beliefs and hopes about what the political system can deliver for them. This goes well beyond the excessive partisanship discussed in the previous chapter. It is about the relationship between politicians and voters – and indeed about the nature of representative democracy itself. Politicians are themselves partly responsible for creating excessive expectations about what they can achieve – which in turn fosters disillusionment about them and their promises. In this chapter, I will discuss, first, the general issue of inflated expectations; second, the specific problem of election promises; and, third, expectations about how MPs should behave.

First, politicians are remarkably bad at explaining what representative democracy is all about and, hence, about what they should and can do. In their public remarks, they are not good at complexity. They tend to talk in simple, unqualified terms. We are right and they are wrong. Because the government is proposing a policy, we, as the opposition, must be against it.

Moreover, as I will discuss later, elections in the age of mass democracy tend to produce inflated promises and expectations wholly at odds with the realities of governing.

That is why I have always disliked the mood of public elation on the Fridays after general elections when there is a change of power. There is something phoney, as well as misleading, about such days. The excitement of the victors and their supporters is understandable, but too often this translates into an absurd and damaging sense of a totally new beginning, as if everything which went before was wrong and can be forgotten. It is not just a question of 'not invented here'. Incoming governments behave as if there has to a fresh start in all policies, so sensible programmes developed by an outgoing government are dropped. History does not end or start on polling day.

After almost every change of party in office, it is only a matter of time before incoming governments revert to some of the policies of their predecessors, having initially rejected them. Sometimes it takes a few years, creating a destabilising interim period for those running the service. In both secondary education and particularly health, the Blair government turned its back on the Major administration's measures to make providers more independent and to introduce limited competition. However, Blair and his advisers regretted their early actions and in the second and third New Labour terms returned to a version of the Major approach in both schools and the NHS. Labour had campaigned during the 1997 election on the absurd and dishonest slogan of twenty, nineteen, eighteen etc. 'days to save the NHS'. The health service certainly had funding problems in the mid-1990s. But talk of 'saving' the NHS was a gross exaggeration which misled voters into thinking that merely changing the government could transform standards of service. It took the Blair government nearly a decade, and big changes in tax and spending policy, and in the organisation of the NHS, before real improvement could be seen, and widely accepted.

The endlessly replayed 'things can only get better' theme of the New Labour campaign in the 1997 election – epitomised by Tony Blair's 'a new dawn is breaking' speech at the Festival Hall on the Friday morning – was catchy, but the opposite of the truth. As Blair himself recognised, and confessed in his frank and self-absorbed autobiography (2010), winning was when the hard bit started. At the opening of his first chapter, Blair describes the emotion of the crowds and throughout the country – 'giving them hope, making them believe all things were possible, that by the very act of election and the spirit surrounding it, the world could be changed'. He says he did not share this emotion: 'my predominant feeling was fear.' He writes about his 'incessant, gnawing desire to get away from the congratulatory euphoria – which I knew would mean little in terms of how we governed – and get down to business'. The mood then was, he says, like 'an oncoming truck', and the public 'weren't troubled by the dilemmas of policymaking or the savage nature of decision-making'. However,

> expectations of this nature cannot be met. That's what you want to tell people. Often you do tell them. But the spirit can't be too constrained. And when finally it departs, leaving your followers with reality – a reality

you have never denied and which you have even sought to bring to their attention – the danger is of disillusion, more painful because of what preceded it.

Blair cannot escape responsibility for raising expectations himself, even though he was – in striking contrast to David Cameron after May 2010 – remarkably cautious. He almost did not believe the scale of his victory in May 1997 and, until far too late in his premiership, was reluctant to take risks on his domestic political agenda. His instinct was to hoard political capital rather than to spend it, for fear that the electorate would turn against him, as it had turned against Labour during the long years of opposition.

Campaigning and governing are very different. The former is about absolute statements; the latter is about relative judgements. In that sense, polling day marks the transition from aspiration to reality. We, the voters, quickly discover that we cannot have everything we want, or believe what politicians have promised us. As Professor Gerry Stoker wrote in his book *Why Politics Matters* (2006): 'The real problem with politics, even in democracies, is that it is inevitably destined to disappoint because it is about the tough process of squeezing collective decisions out of multiple and competing interests and opinions.' Disappointment is inevitable because 'that is the way the process of compromise and reconciliation works. Its outcomes are often messy, ambiguous and never final.'

Professor Matthew Flinders argued in his inaugural lecture (2010) that 'the fact that politics often produces messy compromises; that sub-optional decisions are made and bureaucratic processes appear slow and cumbersome; and that politics inevitably disappoints some sections of the community is simply the price we pay for seeking to govern through consensus'. He notes the use of the term 'expectations gap' by David Miliband when he was director of the Prime Minister's policy unit in the first Blair term – by which he meant the difference between politicians' promises and the public's expectations of what politics and the state could and should deliver, on the one hand, and what politics and the state could realistically deliver given the resources it was provided with, on the other. On this view, politicians should not inflate public expectations.

Politicians seek to mask such a search for compromises by adopting generalised appeals. The rhetoric of One Nation (so beloved of generations of Tory politicians since Disraeli in search of a comforting theme), of the Big Tent (skilfully used to embrace non-Labour politicians and non-political figures by Tony Blair and, less skilfully, by Gordon Brown) and of 'we are all in it together' (the slogan of David Cameron and George Osborne) are irritatingly, and intentionally, vague.

Public expectations can never be fulfilled because the range of hopes and wants is bound to be diverse. Even if we reached the highly improbable situation of having just one economic class – with unified economic interests – there would still be a need to reconcile differences based on age. That most thoughtful of Conservatives, David Willetts wrote a fascinating book, *The Pinch* (2010), on the clash of generations. He focused on the benefits enjoyed by the baby-boomer generation (broadly those born between 1945 and 1965) through mass, and largely free, higher education, rising house prices and increasing real incomes. Those aged over fifty own four-fifths of the nation's wealth. The baby boomers have attained this position at the expense of their children who will face 'the cost of climate change, the cost of investment in the infrastructure our economy will need if we are to prosper, the cost of paying pensions when the big boomer cohort retires, on top of the cost of servicing the debt the government has built up'. (The last point is one of the reasons for incurring short-term pain to eliminate the structural budget deficit in order to reduce the burden, not least of higher taxes, on working people later on.) The baby boomers will live much longer than their own parents' generation born in the first third of the last century, and will impose a burden on their own children's' generation – who will in turn struggle to be able to afford to buy houses and to enjoy rising living standards, as well as having lower social mobility and a degraded environment. Willetts sums up that the charge is 'the boomers have been guilty of a monumental failure to protect the interests of future generations'.

Many of the coalition government's toughest decisions have involved addressing these generational issues – notably on pensions and on tuition fees (where Willetts himself, as Higher Education Minister, was responsible for increasing the amount to be paid by middle income and better off students during their working lives after they graduate). The student finance decision was an inherently political one since it involved reconciling the interests of taxpayers, students (now and in their future lives), and universities. Yet little of the pain will be borne by the baby boomers themselves since they have already enjoyed the benefits of higher education and any changes to pensions will affect those aged below fifty rather than those who have retired, or are about to retire. Such intergenerational issues can only be resolved in a political way by governments balancing out the interests of various groups.

Politicians are also needed as a buffer against the expectations fostered by special interests. With the decline in membership of political parties, pressure groups are able to claim greater legitimacy. One of the clichés of this debate is that the membership of the Royal Society for the Protection of Birds has a larger membership – more than a million – than all political parties put together, while the National Trust has a membership of 3.6 million. So what. Most of the members of the RSPB are making a minimal gesture of mainly financial support for bird protection, while people join the National Trust mainly to have access to their properties. Campaigning organisations such as Friends of the Earth claim large memberships, but again involvement is mainly financial, or through limited email or letter protests. Few of these campaigning groups are genuinely democratic. Their tactics and views on particular issues are generally decided by a small group of full-time organisers. There is nothing wrong with this. These lobbying groups raise important issues and ensure that opinions and interests which would otherwise not be heard have a chance to influence the policy debate.

However, there is a danger that such pressure groups are seen as being more legitimate than they are, or can be. The very term 'non-governmental organisations', or NGOs, raises their status and they are often depicted in the media as having an equal standing to ministers and other representatives of government. This applies particularly in the areas of the environment, international development and human rights where NGOs have become part of the bargaining process, sending larger delegations than many governments to international summits. Their directors are often treated by the media as if they are disinterested, as compared with ministers. This is

grossly misleading. They represent particular and partial interests, which certainly deserve a hearing given their expertise
and knowledge. Their tone can, however, frequently be self-
righteous and dismissive of any other interest or viewpoint.
But, by definition, they are not representative. It is not their
role to take into account other people's interests. That takes
us back again to the argument about the role of politicians
as mediators between such interests and the often unrealistic
expectations of particular pressure groups.

Secondly, there is the specific problem of election promises.
Every government suffers, sooner or later, from charges of
betrayal, either from its more fervent supporters or from the
public. This is a problem both of public expectations and of
politicians' own making. Few politicians are candid ahead of
elections. The most infamous example was Stanley Baldwin's
bold admission in November 1936 about his approach before
the 1935 general election: 'I put before the whole House
my own views with appalling frankness ... supposing that I
had gone to the country and said that we must re-arm, does
anybody think that this pacific democracy would have rallied
to the cry? I cannot think of anything that would have made
the loss of the election from my point of view more certain.'

Few politicians are willing to acknowledge such 'appalling
frankness', yet most are as evasive before elections for similar
reasons. Having reported on ten general elections as a journalist, I cannot remember one when either a government or
an opposition party has been specific about tough economic
measures it might have to take in office – even when their
leaders have known that such action is unavoidable. Never
have I heard a promise to increase interest rates during a campaign – though they have been raised within two months of

polling day after half those elections. And fiscal policy has been tightened through higher taxes and a squeeze on public spending after all but three of the post-election Budgets in that period. But none were quite as flagrant as the turnround from the tax-cutting pre-election Budget of April 1955 to the tax-raising and tightening Budget of October that year in order to remedy some of the earlier damage. This permanently damaged the reputation of R. A. Butler, who was replaced as Chancellor that December by Harold Macmillan, who won the battle for the premiership a little over a year later.

Governing parties naturally behave as if everything is going smoothly and no nasty action will be needed after the election. Opposition parties generally say that the economy is in a mess, but are deliberately vague about what they would do about it. This results in a demeaning game in which the parties challenge each other, aided and abetted by the media, to deny they would put up this or that tax – or face charges that they have a 'secret plan' to do that very thing. These electoral and media pressures mean that parties try and say as little as they can get away with before an election. However, nowadays, they have to say something. That produces two dangers. First, that by ruling out certain tax and spending measures, they will constrain their options in office. Second, they will have to act contrary to their manifesto promises. Both outcomes risk fostering criticism of the sincerity and integrity of politicians.

New Labour faced the first dilemma in opposition, and then at later elections in office. As part of their safety first approach, Tony Blair and Gordon Brown promised they would not raise the basic or higher rates of income tax or extend the scope of VAT. But rates are only one component of what people pay in tax. Rising earnings can push people into higher tax brackets.

Unless the starting thresholds for tax rates are regularly uprated to match the growth in earnings, more people will end up paying more in tax. And there are plenty of other taxes apart from income tax and VAT. Indeed, while Blair and Brown stuck faithfully to their 1997 pledge, which was reiterated at the 2001 and 2005 general elections, they did raise taxes in other ways – both by failing fully to adjust tax thresholds for inflation and by introducing or raising indirect taxes of various kinds. This prompted one of the Conservatives' few telling attacks of this period about 'stealth taxes'. Moreover, in 2002, Brown announced a substantial increase in direct taxes by raising national insurance contributions for both employers and employees. For the latter, a rise in the contribution rate has the same effect as an increase in the basic rate of income tax (though the fully retired without any earnings do not pay NICs). At least initially, Labour got away with this big tax increase since it was tied specifically to additional spending on the NHS. This linkage or earmarking was popular since Brown skilfully made the case for increasing spending (what he called investment) on the NHS. This approach of publicly sticking to manifesto promises, while raising more revenue in other ways, worked until the cataclysm of the 2008 banking crisis when public borrowing soared. The previous tax pledge was broken when a new higher rate of income tax of 50 per cent was introduced, along with a series of other increases in direct tax.

The classic way out of the second dilemma for an opposition party winning an election is to express surprise and shock once they have 'seen the books'. They protest in shocked tones that they had not realised the fiscal position had been allowed to deteriorate so much under their predecessors and was now so bad. So – with deep regret – the incoming government will have to take unpleasant measures to bring borrowing under control. So, unfortunately, they will have to raise taxes and cut spending more than they had hoped before the election. But the real responsibility should lie with the previous governing party. The script is familiar and has been trotted out by virtually every incoming government in my memory. Of course, the Treasury encourages such a blame game since it sees an opportunity both to reassert its influence within Whitehall – which is often on the wane in the more relaxed days before an election – and to press for the fiscal tightening which it instinctively prefers.

On many occasions, there is something in the 'books were worse than we expected' argument. Governing parties invariably avoid hard choices before an election and authorise spending projects in vulnerable constituencies. However, this is seldom secret. The 'books' are no longer a mystery only known to the Treasury.

Outside forecasters – notably organisations such as the Institute of Fiscal Studies – produce pre-election analyses warning about the fiscal position and the tough decisions on spending and tax which will have to be taken by the incoming government. The only people who are reluctant to get too involved in this debate are the government and the main opposition party.

Before the May 2010 election, the IFS warned specifically about the huge fiscal problem which would have to be tackled if borrowing and debt levels were to be brought down to acceptable levels. Even though Alistair Darling, as Chancellor, had been increasingly candid about the extent of the fiscal problem – much to Brown's irritation – his main concern was to ensure that options were not ruled out. Darling resisted pressure from Brown and Ed Balls to rule out a rise in VAT after the election. However, his plans included tens of billions of unspecified spending cuts. On the Conservative side, Cameron and Osborne argued that Labour's published plans would not cut the deficit fast enough, but they tried, not always successfully, to dodge questions about what precisely would be cut. Cameron and his team gave the impression that most of the expenditure savings – note not 'cuts' – could be achieved by eliminating waste and increasing efficiency.

'Our plans involve cutting wasteful spending – our plans don't involve an increase in VAT.' But plans can, and do, change. VAT has been raised, universal child benefit has been cut back for the better off and many programmes face substantial real cuts in expenditure. Osborne has maintained that all this is necessary to eliminate the underlying, structural deficit. His broad argument that drastic action had to be taken over the deficit has been accepted by most voters, even though the specific measures became increasingly unpopular – damaging the standing of the coalition. That has reinforced the image of politicians saying one thing before an election and doing something else afterwards.

At least, the Conservatives' evasions were in anticipation of taking up the responsibilities of office. The Liberal Democrats landed themselves in an even worse position by not taking seriously the possibility of office. They never really took up offers of help and advice in preparing for the possibility of government – a serious challenge for a party none of whose current members had ever held ministerial office. This was in marked contrast to the Conservatives who had prepared their shadow ministers for the possibility of ministerial office through extensive briefings with former civil servants and ex-ministers. The Liberal Democrats mainly concentrated on the politics of a hung parliament, rather than on preparing shadow ministers for the demands of office and of governing. Party leaders did more advanced planning than other parties about possible scenarios in a hung parliament, though most was only in the few months before the election. However, the policy work was weaker. While some of Nick Clegg's advisers had thought about priorities for any coalition negotiations – as David Laws explains in his book (2010) – this did not prevent the party from adopting public policy positions which would soon look unsustainable. In the economic circumstances of spring 2010, it was plain daft for Clegg and his MPs to sign a public pledge during the campaign 'to vote against any increase in (tuition) fees in the next parliament'. Later, the Liberal Democrats argued that, since they had failed to win an outright Commons majority, they could not implement their manifesto commitments and had to reach compromises. That is a credible argument against the absolutists. But the Liberal Democrats knew they would never win an election on their own, and, therefore, compromises would be inevitable in any event if they were to attain their goal of participating in government. The party would have been far better off thinking more about how to achieve some of their policy pledges before putting them in their manifesto. Otherwise, the Liberal Democrats were just inviting the cries of betrayal and the derision which they later faced over the tripling of the maximum tuition fee up to £9,000 – despite all the safeguards introduced to protect poorer students. This was followed by widespread protests by students' organisations and violent street demonstrations in central London from November

2010 onwards. This has been a very painful lesson for the Liberal Democrats about raising false expectations before an election, and has unquestionably damaged the reputation of politicians for honesty.

Politicians should be more candid about the constraints on their freedom of manoeuvre if they win office, and, therefore, more cautious in their promises. This is only partly because of the compromises which are unavoidable in the creation of all coalitions. More often, it is about avoiding promises which are economically unrealistic.

Third, politicians have been seriously damaged by failing to fulfil voters' expectations about their own conduct. Before the cash for questions affair in the mid-1990s, and as lobbying by MPs was on the increase, academic Maureen Mancuso conducted research on the ethical views of MPs (mainly based on interviews in the late 1980s, but published in 1993 and 1995). She showed that: 'The parameters of ethical conduct in the House of Commons remain hazy and blurred. MPs have almost nothing but an unwritten code on which to rely.' In that pre-Nolan era, a full third of those that she interviewed (described as entrepreneurs), were willing to condone almost any activity as long as it did not contravene a written statute or formal rule. This moral permissiveness was, at least partially, shaken by the cash for questions affair and the introduction of a new regime.

The Committee on Standards in Public Life, a new broom responsible for banning lobbying by MPs and tightening up of their outside interests, commissioned some fascinating research into public attitudes, undertaken in 2004, 2006 and 2008 (just before the expenses scandal erupted). This showed that voters said it was extremely important that MPs and ministers should not take bribes, should tell the truth, should make sure that public money is used wisely and should not use their power for their own personal gain (all well above 70 per cent). However, these surveys also revealed serious doubts among voters that not all in public life meet these standards – although that may have been influenced less by personal misconduct than public disillusionment with the Blair government about alleged dissembling over the Iraq War. In 2008, three-fifths of those interviewed said that all or most ministers and MPs did not take bribes. But only just over a fifth said they would trust all or most ministers to tell the truth, and only a quarter said the same about MPs. As Nicholas Allen and Sarah Birch have written in an article on political misconduct and public opinion (2011), the 2008 survey highlighted four areas in which there was a pronounced gap between expectations and perceived behaviour: telling the truth, making sure that public money is used wisely, being in touch with what the general public thinks is important, and owning up to mistakes. This points to a growing public disenchantment with and detachment from ministers and MPs.

Despite this public scepticism about MPs' motives and behaviour, it was, until recently, possible to argue that, as in any institution, there were only a few scoundrels and that, by and large, British public life was pretty clean. As I argued in the previous chapter, I still believe that is still broadly true. But that view is much harder to defend and is not accepted by many voters (even a majority of voters, according to opinion polls). It is not just that some, mainly former, MPs have gone to prison for defrauding the public over their expenses claims, damaging though that is. Nor is it the equally damaging revelations in the

Daily Telegraph in spring 2009 about extravagant claims and the 'flipping' of homes, both which were apparently within the letter, if not the spirit, of the rules.

What has really undermined the standing of politicians has been the values of many MPs which the expenses row has revealed. Sir Christopher Kelly, chairman of the Committee on Standards in Public Life, argued in a speech in May 2010 that

> privately many MPs believed, and still believe, that they are underpaid relative to what they could earn elsewhere, whatever they may say in public. They also think that in recent years their pay has fallen behind some of those in the public sector with whom they used to compare them-selves – GPs, headteachers, police superintendents and so on. Collectively they had allowed their belief to grow into a sense that they were entitled to exploit a generous system of expenses to make up some of the difference. That sense of entitlement was allowed to flourish because of an almost complete lack of transparency and a wholly inadequate system of audit arrangements.

As Sir Christopher argued, that was compounded by a failure of leadership: 'some of those who ought to have been most prominent in maintaining high standards of behaviour in the House, and most zealous in safeguarding its reputation, failed to do so'.

Of course, the small number of prosecutions – and subse-quent prison sentences – have taken the headlines alongside stories about extravagant, though apparently not criminal, claims clearly in abuse of the system. But as worrying has been the moral ambiguity shown by many MPs in conniving at such abuses. As Sir Christopher argued, there was 'a pernicious culture of entitlement' among many MPs. Thanks to a lack of transparency and inadequate audit, this dirty little secret of MPs was maintained until the abuses and flaws in the system were revealed as a result of Freedom of Information legislation, and the *Daily Telegraph*'s disclosures. That combination highlighted the discrepancy in expectations between the public's view of how their MPs ought to behave and how they were shown to have behaved.

That led to an over-reaction as the public appeared hostile to almost any expenses incurred by MPs since a majority believed that MPs were on the fiddle – and that self-righteous tone was adopted by much of the press. The party leaders had hoped that the 2010 general election would mark a turning point as most of the discredited MPs (many disowned by their own parties) left the Commons, while a new, and much tougher, expenses regime was introduced after the election by the Independent Parliamentary Standards Authority (IPSA). However, many MPs resented the new regime, partly because of dislike of the replacement of self-regulation by an independent regulator, and partly because of objections to what were felt to be onerous new rules for expenses. Some members behaved very badly, abusing IPSA's staff. Many MPs argued that these rules failed to take account of their need to maintain homes in London and in their constituencies, involving as they did arbitrary rules about travelling times from Westminster. At the same time, the many new MPs – around two-fifths of the total membership of the Commons – had seen themselves as part of a 'clean' new generation above reproach.

They resented the burden of the rules and what they felt was the implication that any expenses were open to criticism. IPSA became very unpopular among MPs, and, as the coalition's ratings fell in late 2010, David Cameron found that expressing impatience about IPSA was a convenient way of diverting some of the Tory right's criticism away from him. Some of the initial charges against IPSA were fair. The introduction of the new system did have teething problems and the rules were over-complicated, a reaction to the previous lax regime. But as some of the early problems were sorted out, and IPSA substantially revised the expenses rules, the criticisms seemed to be more about the diminished status of MPs themselves as much as the way that IPSA was operating. There was little evidence of public sympathy with MPs. The lack of confidence has fuelled a more general anti-politics, and anti-politician, mood – and will be very hard to repair.

CHAPTER FOUR

TAKING OUT THE POLITICS
– AND THE POLITICIANS

THE ELITE REACTION to the alleged failures of politicians has been to try and depoliticise important issues. A fashionable current of opinion has sought since the 1980s to 'take the politics' out of decisions – whether by setting up arm's-length bodies, by extending the remit and role of the judges, and through various changes intended to shift power from politicians to the People (invariably with a capital P). In this chapter I want to discuss the origins and implications of this desire for depoliticisation. I will examine in later chapters the debates over the role of Parliament and over constitutional reform. Many of these proposals are contradictory and in conflict. For instance, giving responsibility for decisions to arm's-length bodies runs counter to demands for an increased say for voters via direct democracy.

Much of the inspiration behind the 'Big Society' agenda

put forward by David Cameron is not just, or even primarily, to transfer power from central government to local authorities but to transfer decisions out of the hands of politicians entirely and give it to voluntary bodies and individuals. Indeed, local authorities have argued that the sharp cut in central government grants to them risks weakening local democracy, while also inhibiting the growth of voluntary and charitable groups which are heavily dependent on the state for their funds. The 'Big Society' is intended to be about changing the relationship between the state and citizens. In the words of Francis Maude (2010),

> The big government zeitgeist has failed and is over. Top-down micromanagement of public services has made morale plummet and widened inequalities in many areas. Failure to open up the delivery of public services to charities, social enterprises and business has stifled innovation and wasted money. Failure to put power in the hands of communities has meant that people across the country feel excluded from the decision-making process, which in turn undermines social responsibility.

The key is scepticism about the role of the state. So, for all the talk about localism, the 'Big Society' is not primarily about transferring power from central to local government. It is, as David Cameron said (2010),

> about a huge culture change ... where, people in their everyday lives, in their homes, in their neighbourhoods, in their workplace don't always turn to officials, local authorities or central government for answers to the problems they

face, but instead feel both free and powerful enough to help themselves and their own communities … It's about liberation – the biggest, most dramatic redistribution of power from elites in Whitehall to the man and woman on the street.

Stripping away the rhetorical guff, this reflects a profound scepticism about the role not only of the state but also of politicians, and the conventional political process, as opposed to local people and groups. The intention is that ordinary people, not elected politicians, will become the drivers for change and improving standards, both through the provision of more information and, in some cases, by enabling them to set up mutuals and the like to take over local services. But will enough of us become active citizens, or will the main pressures come from self-selecting, and unrepresentative, groups? There is a risk of a vocal and active minority brushing aside the interests of a less active majority. Moreover, even before these plans were implemented, there were concerns at the top of Whitehall that they risk eroding the basic principles of transparency and ministerial accountability. Ministers argue that their insistence on the publication of the full details of spending above a specified low amount will ensure that voters and local groups will be able to hold providers of services to account. The critics fear, however, that outsourcing services to charities and the private sector may make it harder to find out how money is being spent, as well as undermining accountability to Parliament. The National Audit Office has warned that changes to the structure of the NHS, decentralising budgetary control to local GPs, could reduce ministerial accountability. In all, these changes could, and are partly intended to, make politicians less central to key decisions on the provision of services affecting all voters.

Within the whole depoliticisation debate, there is an underlying thread of suspicion of politicians. Party politics is seen as having an inherent tendency towards self-seeking, and even at times corrupt, behaviour and a short-term perspective which is inimical to sound long-term public policy. This is similar, if less crude, than the view of the populists: a mistrust of politicians, their ambitions and behaviour. Put at a more elevated level, the often-heard jibe that they 'are all in it for themselves' translates into the public choice theories of members of the Virginia school of political economy such as James Buchanan and Gordon Tullock. According to them, politicians and bureaucrats (and the latter pejorative phrase is always used) are not disinterested, but, like the rest of us, have their own interests such as patronage, power, perks and pay which influence how they spend our, the taxpayers', money.

This is a fundamental ideological debate between those who want to rein back the state and those who believe the effect of privatisation and liberalisation has been to narrow what they call the 'public realm'. To democratic socialist thinkers, such as David Marquand (2004), the effect of the pro-market policies of the Thatcher government – largely endorsed by New Labour and intensified by the Conservative–Liberal Democrat coalition – has been to undermine the ethos of public service. The collectivist values of equity, fairness and equality nurtured in the 1940s were replaced by those of the free market – the individual and choice.

The academic argument is that there are deep, innate differences between the public and private sectors in their values and behaviour. Professor Flinders argued (2010) that 'the marketisation and commodification of the state played a key role in undermining public confidence in politics. It emphasised individualism, personal choice and material benefits while doing little to foster those facets of collective behaviour (the public sector ethos, citizenship, institutional memory etc.) that had taken half a century to build.' In particular, the notion of the citizen consumer nurtured by the Thatcherite and Blairite reforms had encouraged people to demand levels of service provision that would commonly be provided only in the private sector, but 'thereby inflating public expectations far beyond what the state or politics was intended, expected or resourced to provide'. This clash of cultures, between the individual and the collective, is seen as challenging the scope for political argument and for politicians.

But this argument should not be exaggerated. The critics of the extension of free markets are themselves involved in a political debate, just as much as the advocates of rolling back the state and increasing personal choice are. Thatcher was no less a politician engaged in political debate and conduct than Attlee was. Here too there are contradictions. Some of those on the centre-left who want to defend the traditional role of politicians as protectors of the 'public realm' by limiting the encroachment of markets into public services often want, at the same time, to constrain those very politicians by extending direct democracy.

Depoliticisation emerged as a major theme during the 1980s and 1990s. In part, it was ideological, a reflection of the debates among economists about how to produce financial stability after more than a decade of rising inflation and sluggish growth. A common argument in this period was that the pressures of the electoral cycle led politicians to take short-term decisions to increase public spending and cut taxes ahead of elections which were economically damaging and stoked up inflation. Politicians could not be trusted to behave responsibly and therefore they should be constrained by formal rules. The first experiments in what turned out to be called monetarism turned out to have mixed results as the money supply proved very hard to control.

Similarly, the attempt by the Thatcher government from 1980 onwards to bring down both monetary growth and the level of public borrowing through firm targets set out in the medium-term financial strategy proved to be anything but smooth because of cyclical pressures. As Miss Prism would undoubtedly have said, this subject, like the chapter on the Fall of the Rupee, may be 'somewhat too sensational' for the current volume – and anyone wanting to pursue this argument can look at my earlier books: *The Thatcher Government* (1983) and *The Thatcher Era and its Legacy* (1991).

Yet the desire to insulate key economic decisions from electoral and political pressures by adopting firm monetary anchors continued in the late 1980s and early 1990s, initially through Britain's ill-fated membership from 1990 until 1992 of the exchange rate mechanism of the European Monetary System (the ERM), and then in the debate over the euro. After Black Wednesday, in September 1992, when sterling was forced out of the ERM, politicians sought to establish market credibility and confidence by adopting a public target for inflation, and making decision-making increasingly explicit. The logical extension of this rules-based approach was the Labour government's decision in May 1997, only days after winning the general election, to make the Bank of England operationally responsible for setting interest rates via the creation of the Monetary Policy Committee (MPC). This, the first, most important, and successful, announcement by Gordon Brown as Chancellor was specifically intended to insulate such decisions from politicians and electoral and political pressures. He later made a point of saying that as Chancellor he was not involved in interest rate decisions.

This was in marked contrast to the days when I was an economics correspondent during the tumultuous period from 1976 to 1981, when the process was far from transparent and interest rate decisions were taken by the Chancellor in close consultation with the Governor. I would regularly have a late afternoon phone conversation on Wednesdays with the Bank spokesman, then the dryly humorous and conscientious Brian Quinn – who in retirement became chairman of Celtic football club. Brian would hint – though never explicitly – which way the decision might go as if the movement of the Governor's eyebrows (then the famously enigmatic Gordon Richardson) could be communicated down a phone line. And I had the duty of interpreting this on the front page of the *Financial Times* to the world's financial markets. This was a great opportunity for me as a journalist, but it was inferior in every way to the current open and transparent system. Indeed, the old, close relationships of trust would never have survived the arrival of 24-hour news and a proliferation of instant financial news websites.

Under the post-1997 system, the Chancellor set an inflation target which was reviewed every year, and the MPC was free to adjust interest rates to meet it. As I discuss in the later chapter on Parliament, accountability has been ensured by the regular appearance of the Bank Governor and members of the MPC in front of the Treasury Committee of the Commons, as well as by the publication of the detailed minutes of the monthly meetings of the MPC. Fortunately the economic background was benign for the first decade of the new system. The key to the success of Bank independence in political terms was that the target was straightforward, so the MPC was given a clear-cut task, at least until the autumn of 2008 when the banking crisis erupted which initiated a bout of deflation.

Fiscal policy has proved to be much harder to depoliticise. This is partly because there are more variables affecting the levels of spending and taxation and many of the decisions are inherently more controversial and partisan than over the implementation of inflation targets. The imposition of firm fiscal rules on levels of borrowing, and hence indirectly on spending, in order to constrain the freedom of manoeuvre of politicians has not worked well. In the USA, the Gramm-Rudman-Hollings Balanced Budget Act in 1985 setting firm fiscal targets failed to prevent a rise in the Federal Budget deficit in the face of adverse economic pressures, as well as electoral and political ones, to spend more. Despite later revision, the deficit target was abandoned and replaced within five years. Balanced budgets did not eventually emerge until the late 1990s, and then were short-lived. Moreover, in Britain, as was shown during the election debates in 2010, decisions over the level of the Budget deficit, and the speed of reducing it, are inherently matters for political decision. They cannot be delegated to a non-partisan, and depoliticised, body like the MPC.

However, the attraction of trying to depoliticise economic decision-making has remained. There has, for instance, been the partly proven suspicion that ministers have influenced the Treasury's economic analyses and forecasts. Hence George

Osborne, in opposition, proposed the creation of the Office for Budget Responsibility (OBR) to prepare half-yearly assessments of growth and deficit prospects. As noted in the next chapter on Parliament, the OBR's independence was underpinned by the Treasury Committee of the Commons being given a role in the appointment and re-appointment of its members. By providing forecasts at one remove from the Treasury, the OBR can monitor the rate of progress towards achieving fiscal targets and other economic indicators. But it is for the Chancellor to set those fiscal targets, and to decide on the balance between public spending and taxation measures.

Brown also became keen to extend this principle to other areas such as decisions on takeovers by creating the Competition Commission, though ministers had to decide whether to accept a proposal to refer a bid to it. A similar approach lay behind the formation of the Infrastructure Planning Commission to decide on major transport, airport and energy projects, such as civil nuclear power stations, in line with criteria approved by Parliament.

In parallel, there was a largely administrative drive from the late 1980s onwards to devolve responsibility for the implementation of policy to semi-independent executive agencies. This was motivated partly by the belief that management would be better if their day-to-day running were removed from the hands of ministers, and hence insulated from short-term political pressures. There was a strong case for doing this for well-defined administrative tasks such as running job centres and issuing passports. In the mid-1990s attempts were made to distinguish between policy (the role of ministers) and administration (that of officials). But the lines proved hard to maintain when things went wrong. Ministers were expected to explain what had happened, and what was being done to remedy matters, the *Today* programme test of political accountability.

The proliferation of arm's-length bodies of various kinds – from executive agencies working within government to non-departmental public bodies with independent heads and often their own distinctive public profile and voice – has produced a counter-reaction over the past decade. There have been complaints about unelected bodies not being properly accountable to voters. There are interesting cross-currents here: just at a time when politicians are being criticised as a class, so there are attempts to bring back public activities within the direct realm of political debate.

The Conservative–Liberal Democratic coalition government came to power pledging to cut the number of such unelected quangos. David Cameron said in July 2009 when outlining this proposal in opposition that: 'Our starting presumption is a preference for democratic accountability over bureaucratic accountability. That means that wherever possible, we will expect ministers to exercise their responsibility through their departments.' This was partly on the grounds that various public bodies had been set up in the past in order to avoid ministers having to take responsibility for difficult decisions. Francis Maude, the Cabinet Office Minister responsible for the review of arm's-length bodies in the coalition, argued that the case for bringing bodies back rested on the primacy of Parliament as a forum for accountability. But as a Public Administration Committee report in January 2011 (revealingly entitled 'Smaller Government: Shrinking the Quango State') argued, the arguments are, in practice, more complicated.

The mere structure of an arm's-length body with a board

and chief executive publicly answerable for decisions would ensure as much, if not more, public accountability than traditional ministerial accountability to Parliament.

The Institute for Government in its 2010 report on this issue, 'Read before Burning', argues that:

> Arm's-length bodies are not as exempt from blame and sanction as commentators sometimes suggest. Indeed, non-departmental public body chairs often argue that they are in practice much more accountable than their civil service counterparts. They are accountable to the department and the minister, they can be summoned to appear before a select committee, and while civil servants are rarely named and can take refuge behind the doctrine of ministerial responsibility, ALB chairs and chief executive officers appear in the media in their own right and can carry the can for their decisions.

There is a strong case for keeping some bodies at arm's length, notably those where a degree of independence from day-to-day ministerial intervention is desirable so that they can demonstrate political impartiality and command public confidence. This applies especially to those bodies which scrutinise government and exercise regulatory functions, such as the Judicial Appointments Commission, the Crown Prosecution Service, the Competition Commission and the Office of Fair Trading (the latter two being merged). The PASC report fairly accused the government of inconsistency in its approach.

This debate has tended to be muddled by the use of the word 'unelected' as a term of abuse, as if only those who have been elected to the Commons and become ministers should be in direct charge of any government operation. For a start, that excludes the many ministers in the Lords with responsible positions in government departments. But government is so large and complicated that ministers cannot possibly run everything. The key is to have robust account-ability mechanisms to ensure that ministers are answerable to elected representatives of voters, namely MPs, to explain how parts of government are run, and to provide explanations if anything goes wrong.

Depoliticisation has also seen the involvement of 'impartial' experts to provide non-political cover for what you want to do. If Sir X, a man of impeccable authority, thinks this is the right course of action, than all right-thinking people must agree, and we should do it. No matter that other Sir Ys and Sir Zs, also of impeccable authority, might recommend an entirely different course of action. Increasingly in the last few years we have seen the appointment of tsars to advise on this or that area of government, from drugs to cancer via homelessness and social exclusion. These hybrid figures are not permanent civil servants nor are they special advisers. Their usefulness lies in their reputation and expertise. They help give politicians credibility in tackling a problem. But such appointments often end unhappily as the tsars are torn between their professional commitment to evidence and the political demands of their ministerial masters. Such has been the unhappy fate of drug advisers in the face of pressures for a tough stance.

Gordon Brown – that most acute of politicians in analysing currents of opinion, if not in communicating them – was par-ticularly fond of appointing non-political businessmen to carry out reviews. This matched his liking for depoliticising some sensitive decisions, like interest rates. Every spring Budget or autumn Pre-Budget Report Brown made as Chancellor usually included the announcement of a new review. The litany of names (Atkinson, Barker, Clementi, Cruickshank, Gershon, Hampton, Higgs, Lambert, Lyons, Miles, Pickering, Sandler, Taylor, Turner and Wanless) reads like a Gilbert and Sullivan patter song. And many of these reviews were impressive analyses of the issues covered. For Brown, however, they were mainly useful to provide impartial and authoritative justification for measures he wanted to introduce – and in some cases would anyway have introduced. Those reports which produced politically awkward recommendations were generally soon forgotten. The most important use of an outside businessmen to provide cover for a major policy change was the review by Sir Derek Wanless, a senior bank executive, of NHS funding The Wanless review appeared in two stages. The first interim report in November 2001 identified a big funding gap between planned resources and demands from an ageing population, technological changes and rising public expectations. The second, and final, report in April 2002, examined and dismissed alternatives to a taxpayer-funded system. This enabled Brown to announce both a big rise in public spending and an increase in taxes (in the form of higher employer and employee national insurance contributions). These were the largest tax rises before the banking and economic crisis hit in 2008. Brown mentioned Wanless repeatedly in his April 2002 Budget speech – almost as if his name were like a magic potion – in order to justify this substantial change in policy.

Brown continued this approach when he became Prime Minister in June 2007. He not only extended the Big Tent political approach of Blair – by seeking to appoint political opponents to important public positions, such as his unsuccessful wooing of Paddy Ashdown to join his Cabinet, But, and the distinction is not always appreciated, he also sought distinguished non-political figures to become ministers principally because they had a reputation and experience outside politics. These were the 'Goats' – the government of all the talents – including a leading doctor, Lord Darzi, a prominent former journalist and international diplomat Lord Malloch-Brown, a former First Sea Lord in Lord West, and a former director-general of the Confederation of British Industry in Lord (Digby) Jones. They were followed by others during the Brown premierships, such as Lord (Mervyn) Davies, the banker, and Lord Myners, a company chairman. Their appeal was precisely because they were not seen as partisan or political figures. This approach has continued under David Cameron with the appointment of two leading City figures, Lords Sassoon and Green, to become a Treasury minister and Trade minister respectively.

Depoliticisation has also emerged as a direct response to scandals involving politicians. The cash for questions affair in the mid-1990s led, as noted in earlier chapters, to the creation of the Committee on Standards in Public Life in 1994, initially under the late Lord Nolan, as a permanent watchdog on ethical standards. Its first report in 1995 resulted in a tightening up of the rules on MPs' outside interests and creation of the Parliamentary Commissioner for Standards to investigate complaints; a later report was followed by a far-reaching overhaul of electoral law with much greater disclosure of both expenditure and donations and the creation of the Electoral Commission. The expenses row in 2009 led to the creation of the Independent Parliamentary Standards Authority and a much tighter regime of expenses.

In each of these cases, the previously closed world of politicians and parties has been challenged by the creation of semi-independent advisers and agencies. While the Commons retains the final say over disciplining its members, via the cross-party Standards and Privileges Committee, and ultimately votes on the floor of the House, investigations are conducted by the arm's-length Parliamentary Commissioner. He or she is not completely independent as Elizabeth Filkin discovered when her assiduity annoyed many MPs, including Betty Boothroyd, the then Speaker of the Commons, ruling out any chance of a second term.

Belatedly, following a series of scandals about lobbying and a failure to declare outside interests, the House of Lords modified its previous system of investigation by a committee of peers and its senior clerk by appointing its own Commissioner for Standards.

The creation of IPSA has, as discussed in an earlier chapter, replaced internal procedures under the control – and, more to the point, day-to-day influence – of MPs. IPSA's rules-based system has proved very controversial with MPs, who both object to the procedures and to the impact of the regulation and the form filling on them. These changes, taken as a whole, have been intended to ensure transparency in financial arrangements and to try and persuade the public that any complaints are being investigated properly. This has only brought Parliament into line with the compliance and ethics regimes of most outside large organisations. But the underlying assumption, certainly in the eyes of much of the media, is that MPs cannot be trusted on their own and require outside regulators to police their activities.

Many MPs and peers, however, resent these changes as

undermining the sovereignty of Parliament and the principle of self-regulation. It is no good saying that MPs should be judged solely by their constituents at the time of each general election. Unless externally monitored information is available about MPs' conduct and financial position, voters will be unable to form any judgement about their representatives. Similarly, traditional appeals to honour in the Lords are no longer sufficient in view of repeated, though admittedly isolated, scandals and clearly flawed systems for payments. As noted earlier, the public, reinforced by the press, has scant sympathy with the complaints of parliamentarians and would favour even more stringent controls.

However, the behaviour of some MPs and peers, and the repeated weaknesses of their own internal systems, has made the existence of such outside watchdogs and regulators inevitable.

The prevailing view is that politicians can no longer be trusted to police their own affairs and regulation should be taken out of their hands.

The mid-1990s' ethical reforms did not just affect politicians and parties. Responding to claims about partisan political patronage in public appointments, the Committee on Standards on Public Life proposed new rules for how people are appointed to various public bodies. But this has produced undesirable side effects. Obviously, public appointments should be decided on merit and suitability. But, too often, there has been an underlying assumption that anyone with political experience is tainted. The headhunters involved in helping to narrow down the number of candidates, as well as the final selection panels, are liable to play safe, and to tick boxes. This can produce identikit appointees – similar to the people who are appointing them – excluding people with relevant experience in the murky world of achieving compromises known as politics. The Electoral Commission began by excluding both commissioners and staff with any remotely recent party involvement. But this opened the commission up to widely held complaints that it was too detached and ignorant of the day-to-day world of running parties and elections. The earlier ruling has been partially relaxed and amending legislation has resulted in the appointment of some commissioners nominated by the parties. It remains to be seen, however, what happens when an allegation directly affecting the party comes before the commission.

This chapter shows the difficulties involved in depoliticisation. In many areas, there is a strong case for removing politicians from direct day-to-day responsibility – for instance, for many regulators where impartiality is required – but it is usually an illusion to believe that an issue can be taken out of politics. While the creation of the Office for Budget Responsibility to provide independent forecasts and monitoring of government policies on deficit reduction is sensible, the basic decisions on the necessary spending and tax measures have to be taken by politicians. The search for single right and impartial solutions above politics is illusory. There are bound to be disagreements on grounds of ideology, class, interest and, increasingly, age (those still earning versus the retired), and politics, and politicians, exist to reconcile these differences.

CHAPTER FIVE

PARLIAMENT – THE
STIRRING GIANT

THESE CHALLENGES ARE linked to the widely held, but grossly-oversimplified, view that Parliament is in decline – and that politicians are ineffective as well as self-seeking and corrupt. Backbench MPs are dismissed as just lobby fodder, subservient to an all-powerful executive – which is incidentally dominated by the same elected politicians in their roles as ministers. Hence, members of the Commons are regarded as largely irrelevant, compared with ministers and external corporate influences. As I argued in Chapter One, this is a familiar complaint, heard over the centuries, but particularly since the arrival of the mass franchise.

This argument also confuses the true role of Parliament. In Gladstone's famous phrase, 'the business of the House of Commons is not to run the country, but to call to account those who do'. Definitions of what this means in practice have evolved considerably since Gladstone said these words over 150 years ago. He adopted a narrow definition strictly limiting inquiries by Commons committees. But the principle is clear. The test for Parliament is how rigorously and effectively it scrutinises the actions of government. Both the Commons and Lords perform better than is generally appreciated outside Westminster but they still under-perform compared to what they should be doing.

At present, the balance is tilted in favour of the executive and against the legislature and the elected representatives of the public. This is partly because the procedures of the Commons give advantages to ministers in their control over time, as they have for more than a century. Despite recent changes in the control over backbenchers' debates, government business still has priority on most days, reinforced by devices such as programme motions limiting the time for debates on legislation.

Moreover, as I have written before (1998), the past centrality of Parliament as an arena for political debate has been under challenge from a variety of constitutional and social changes, such as devolution to Scotland, Wales and Northern Ireland; from membership of the European Union (whose laws override those passed by the Westminster Parliament in cases of conflict); and, as discussed in a later chapter, from a shifting of responsibility to an increasingly assertive judiciary and arm's-length regulators. The latter changes reflect a suspicion of politicians and a desire to limit their discretion.

Broadcasting studios, the internet and even to some extent newspapers have replaced the floor of the Commons as arenas for political debate in ways which would be thought unimaginable, as well as undesirable, for politicians of the Churchill and Attlee generation, as discussed in Chapter Seven. During the banking crisis of autumn 2008, Alistair Darling made many of his important announcements on the *Today* programme on Radio 4, partly to ensure that the decisions were known ahead of the opening of the London stock market, and a few hours later repeated them on the floor of the Commons, when they made much less impact. Despite frequent tut-tutting, and promises by all incoming governments of making statements first in the Commons, accountability to media interviewers generally comes ahead of accountability to elected politicians.

Yet the declinist thesis is vastly exaggerated and wrong in many respects. Parliament is still the main means by which governments seek to enact, or to defend, their policies – and politicians are obviously crucial to both. Moreover, an already effective and vibrant committee system has recently been strengthened in ways which tend to be ignored, if appreciated at all, by those who regard Parliament as irrelevant. Indeed, despite the increased number and prominence of outsiders brought in as ministers in the Lords (highlighted by Gordon Brown's mixed bag of 'goats'), conventional politicians remain dominant in all governments, holding most ministerial posts. They may be disliked and criticised, but they retain the levers of power as ministers.

Moreover, the critics are wrong about the alleged ineffectiveness of the current generation of MPs. A frequently heard claim – particularly during the Blair/Brown years – from both the *Daily Mail/Daily Telegraph* right and the Channel Four/ Our Kingdom website left is that Parliament has been substantially weakened in the past two decades, especially since 1997, by the combination of an over-mighty and arrogant executive and a weak legislature. This view was typified by the deeply flawed and often ill-informed report of the Power Inquiry of March 2006, chaired by Baroness (Helena) Kennedy, which has been subject to coruscating analysis from several political scientists, and I discuss this in more detail in the next chapter. The Power report concluded that: 'The executive in Britain is now more powerful in relation to Parliament than it has probably been since the time of Walpole. The whips have enforced party discipline more forcefully and fully than they did in the past.' A similar error was made by Roy Hattersley when, in 2005, he described Labour backbenchers as 'the most supine MPs in British history'. These themes have been echoed from the right: even columnists with considerable historical knowledge such as Simon Heffer (of the *Daily Mail*, and now back at the *Daily Telegraph*) talked of the Commons adopting 'a posture of slavishness and ineffectuality'. He also complained about how the Blair government had emasculated the House of Lords by the removal of most hereditary peers and by the creation of many new Labour ones.

The weakness of Parliament, and especially the Commons, has also been cited by many of the older establishment, retired senior civil servants and the like, who set up the Better Government Initiative to campaign for improvements in both Whitehall and Westminster. Sir Christopher Foster, a government adviser during the 1970s and 1980s, has been the prime mover behind the BGI. His book *British Government in Crisis* (2005) highlighted a decline in parliamentary accountability. Many of the BGI's specific proposals – for example for improving the way that Bills are drafted, explained and then considered – are sensible and overdue. But the underlying assumptions often smack too much of a 'better yesterday' attitude – 'we did it better in our day' – which takes too rosy a view of the past record. Procedures of Cabinet government may have been more scrupulously observed in the 1970s but the outcomes, particularly the performance of the economy and of governments generally, were pretty mediocre.

Many of these criticisms were triggered by a strong dislike of Tony Blair, and particularly his handling of the Iraq War, and the alleged inadequacies of parliamentary scrutiny of his actions and statements. In reality, the Commons was informed regularly, although, as we now know, patchily, partially and inadequately, about the intelligence and legal aspects during the run-up to the war. But, far from being supine, as Lord Hattersley alleged two years later, February and March 2003 saw two of the largest revolts ever by government backbenchers against such an important policy. This was the massive, living contradiction of lazy talk about lobby fodder. Consequently, it is misleading to look at the record of MPs and the Commons just, or primarily, through the prism of the Iraq War.

The critics are wrong in their view of both the past and the present. Admittedly, debates were better attended forty or fifty years ago; even thirty years ago when I first reported the Commons, the final or wind-up speeches to debates (then generally from 9.30pm until 10pm) were not only well-attended but ministers occasionally made announcements – so journalists had to be on alert. In the autumn of 1987, a Treasury minister announced the sale of the government's remaining share stake in BP at about 9.45pm, and I had fifteen minutes to dictate a story straight into the telephone to a copytaker for what became the splash or lead story in the next day's *Financial Times* – a period piece in every aspect. But these events, however memorable as theatre or journalistic nostalgia, were deceptive. Despite higher attendance in the chamber, and greater reporting of what they said, backbenchers had much less influence thirty or forty years ago than now.

The declinists like to talk about the independent-minded backbenchers of the past, Tory members who 'had had a good war' and Labour MPs who had real experience of the world on the coalface or shipyard. These are contrasted with the professional career politicians of today who have known nothing but politics as researchers and special advisers before entering the Commons. The social and career background of the Commons has changed with a largely private sector middle class facing a mainly public sector middle class. But the effect on behaviour has been the opposite of what the critics claim. Back in the 1950s, there were two whole parliamentary sessions when not a single government backbencher defied the party whip, including 1956–57, when the Suez debacle unfolded. That began to change after 1970. As, first, Professor Philip Norton and, more recently, Professor Philip Cowley and Mark Stuart have documented, the scale and frequency of rebellions has increased over the past four decades – and particularly since 1997. The Iraq debates, noted above, when record numbers of MPs voted against their party whip in opposing military action (mainly Labour members but also a minority of Tories), were obviously crucial. But even before then, Labour members had begun voting against the Blair government.

And once an MP starts to vote against their party, he or she is more likely to be a repeat offender. In the past, new MPs have taken time to start rebelling, more likely after a year or two in the Commons. However, after the 2010 election, and the formation of the coalition, new Tory MPs started defying the party whip within weeks and months of being elected, in most cases claiming that they were defending party principles against dilution by the alliance with the Liberal Democrats. This has already made the first session of the 2010 parliament the most rebellious ever.

This change may be partly a reflection of the rise of the career politician since – contrary to the fashionable criticism of a professional political class – such MPs are less naturally obedient than the old-style officer class or trade unionists. (I will discuss later in the book whether, and how, the background of MPs should, and can, be broadened.) The younger generation of MPs are much more active, both in their constituencies and at Westminster. One of the paradoxes of the low standing of MPs in general is that most members are far more active in handling constituents' complaints than in the past. Some more senior MPs are worried that they are spending too much time on their welfare officer role and not enough as parliamentarians at Westminster. But it is very hard for an MP to say to a worried constituent, go away and talk to your local councillor who is responsible for housing, refuse, schools or whatever. That is not the way to win votes. At Westminster, the career politicians are reluctant to be merely passive bystanders and they are less afraid of expressing themselves and of defying their party whips, particularly on issues such as Europe since the early 1990s for Tory MPs and opposition to welfare cuts for Labour members.

This applies particularly to those who have no ministerial ambitions or, even more serious for the government whips, those who have been passed over for office, or later in the life of a government have been dropped as ministers. I have hardly ever known a former minister who has been sacked (as opposed to leaving voluntarily) who has not harboured some resentment against the Prime Minister who got rid of him or her. Many such ex-ministers become receptive to the idea of rebellion. As Margaret Thatcher, John Major and Tony Blair all found, the number of potential rebels increases with every reshuffle.

The impact of such rebellions is not just on the rare occasions when the government is defeated – thought this happened four times for the Blair administration in the long first session after the 2005 election – but more in the anticipatory action of ministers to avoid such losses or even close shaves. No government wants a permanent core of disaffected backbenchers, not least because an impression of disunity damages a ruling party's electoral prospects. So ministers, through the whips and their parliamentary private secretaries, seek to take on board, and if possible accommodate, the concerns of backbench MPs. Policy is modified, and amendments to Bills introduced to avoid defeats. In a revealing coincidence, the political weakness of both the Major and Brown governments was shown when Bills to introduce private capital into the Royal Mail were dropped because of the threat of backbench opposition.

Similarly, the House of Lords has turned into a far more effective and assertive chamber – and a troublesome one for the government since the departure of most of the hereditary peers in 1999. This was despite the large number of new creations which made Labour the largest single party (just) in the chamber (though well short of an overall majority). Labour could be easily outvoted when the Conservatives and Liberal Democrats voted together, regardless of the votes of crossbench/independent peers (who, anyway, have a much lower turnout on a day-to-day basis). The Labour government suffered twice as many defeats in the years after 1999 as in the period before then. Moreover, as Meg Russell, the leading authority on the behaviour of the modern Lords, has pointed out, it is not just the increased frequency of defeats, it is also that a significant proportion (around two-fifths) stick and are not reversed. The explanation is that, before 1999, the predominantly hereditary Lords exercised considerable restraint over defeating government measures, though Labour claimed this restraint was discriminatory against its governments.

But the removal of all but ninety-two of the hereditaries legitimised the predominantly appointed House, which has felt emboldened to challenge the Commons, or rather the government of the day, much more than in the pre-1999 era. The Lords has anyway increasingly consisted of active peers (both life and hereditary) committed to their work there. This has been seen not only in the scrutiny of legislation but also in the network of committees, though, as I will discuss later in the book, neither are quite as good as the champions of the Lords like to claim, and are certainly capable of improvement.

The formation of the coalition has created a theoretical working majority in the Lords for the combined Conservative–Liberal Democrat forces over Labour, as happened in December 2010 in the controversial vote on raising the upper limit for tuition fees. But it has not turned out that way on all issues. Some Conservative peers have rebelled, or abstained, either in person or by not turning up. At the same time, an increasingly assertive Labour group – and notably its vocal ex-MP contingent – has found sufficient allies on the crossbenches to defeat the coalition on some of its contentious constitutional Bills, notably the measure to make it easier to abolish some arm's-length bodies through secondary legislation.

As important as the change in the voting behaviour of MPs and peers have been reforms in procedures which have shifted the balance between the legislature and the executive. The shift towards strengthening Parliament has so far been limited and has not gone nearly far enough – notably in the scrutiny of legislation, as successive Hansard Society reports (1993, 2008 and 2010) have highlighted, as I discuss in a later chapter. But the Commons and Lords are now both very different from forty or fifty years ago. The scrutiny role has been strengthened in several stages:

• first, through the replacement of a piecemeal system of monitoring of the executive by the creation in 1979 of select committees. These look at all the main departments, with a gradual extension to cover gaps and to match mergers and break ups of departments;

• second, the agreement in the 2001–05 parliament on giving committees core tasks (scrutiny of government legislation, of administration and the performance of government departments, of public expenditure plans, and of major public appointments), with annual reports on their activities, the creation of a specialist Scrutiny Unit to provide more advice, the start of extra payments for committee chairmen, and the twice yearly questioning of the Prime Minister by members of the Liaison Committee, consisting of the chairmen of all the select committees;

• third, the greater independence of select committees following the decision, made after the 2010 election, to have their chairs elected by all MPs, and their other members by party groups. This has reduced the influence of the party whips and has allowed committee chairs to be more independent;

• fourth, the creation after the 2010 election of a Backbench Business Committee to select topics for debate on thirty-five days during the long post-election session, including at least twenty-seven in the main chamber. This means virtually every Thursday there is a debate on a substantive motion chosen openly from a range of proposals put forward by backbenchers, when previously government business managers and the whips would have picked the subject. The result has been lively and vigorous debates on issues such as Afghanistan (the first on a substantive motion), on contaminated blood and on the future of IPSA, all of which have challenged the government. A select committee chairman has also been given a slot to outline, and be questioned on, the main points of a new report. This could also be the means by which issues raised in public petitions could be debated. The coalition is committed to introducing a full Business Committee by the end of 2013 to allocate time for all debates.

The last two changes were introduced following a special committee inquiry in the summer and autumn of 2009 headed by Tony Wright, the former Labour MP, which was set up in the wake of the expenses scandal to consider Commons reform. The overall impact of all these changes has been considerable. Admittedly, select committees vary enormously in their assiduity and effectiveness, depending in large part on the attitudes and often idiosyncrasies of their chairs. A persistent problem has been the executive mindedness of MPs. A depressing development in October 2010 was how so many newly elected MPs left select committees barely three months after being elected to them and became, alternatively, either parliamentary private secretaries to ministers on the government side or junior opposition spokesmen in Ed Miliband's new Labour team. Of course, this does not prevent them speaking in the Commons chamber on subjects outside their departmental briefs but it has taken some of the most talented new MPs off the select committees before they have had any chance to learn about scrutiny. It is perhaps naive to hope that Prime Ministers and Leaders of the Opposition will voluntarily agree not to make such appointments for the first two years of a parliament. At present, the Commons loses, and, over the longer-term, so do many of these MPs promoted too soon.

However, senior ministers and civil servants now face much closer scrutiny on their performance, policies and proposals than they ever did prior to 1979. The eventual reports, in general, matter less than the public, and now often televised, sessions when witnesses are questioned. Consequently, most major issues or scandals are at least examined by MPs – from the aftermath of the banking crisis of autumn 2008 to recurrent problems of defence procurement and the shortcomings of the criminal justice system. A good example of the system working well has been over monetary policy. After the Bank of England was given operational responsibility for setting interest rates in 1997, Giles (now Lord) Radice, then chairman of the Treasury Committee, tried unsuccessfully to get the subsequent legislation amended to give MPs a say over appointments to its key Monetary Policy Committee (MPC). In the absence of a formal confirmation power, as in the US

Senate, he initiated appointment hearings for new members after their appointment. These became part of a regular annual cycle of hearings when the Governor and senior members of the MPC have been questioned about its Inflation Report. This has helped to transform the accountability of the Bank of England and to ensure that the Governor and members of the MPC have to explain their thinking and policies publicly, rather than hide behind the opaque statements of the past.

In the summer of 2010, Tory MP Andrew Tyrie, the first chairman of the Treasury Committee elected by the whole House, demonstrated his independence by persuading George Osborne to allow the committee a veto not only over the appointment of members of the new Office for Budget Responsibility but also over their reappointment and hence dismissal. This was seen as a protection against any Treasury attempt to curtail the tenure of an OBR member whose fore-casts and analysis were not to its liking. It was immediately emphasised that this was not a precedent for granting other Commons committees a veto over public appointments even though, in some cases, they would have a consultative role. This is a tricky area: how far should the legislature become involved in appointments by having a veto power, as opposed to just scrutinising the suitability of appointees?

This episode highlights many of the tensions at the heart of Commons reform. None of the changes has happened easily. Reform has depended on fortuitous timing, often at the start of parliaments and when there is a reform-minded Leader of the Commons – notably Robin Cook in the 2001–03 period, though he faced obstruction from the party whips and allies of Gordon Brown. Mr Cook started with reformist instincts, strengthened by demands for change frustrated under his predecessor. That was Margaret Beckett, instinctively more conservative, and more party and executive minded. Mr Cook also had the advantage of a ready-made blueprint for change in the form of a series of recommendations for strengthening select committees made by a Hansard Society Commission, chaired by Tony Newton, a former Leader of the Commons, of which I was a vice-chairman. ('The Challenge for Parliament – Making Government Accountable', 2001). Greg Power, the commission's secretary, became one of Mr Cook's special advisers.

The debates over reform have reflected a continued tension between the executive, in particular the party whips, and reform-minded members of the Commons (with parallel tensions in the much slower moving Lords). The whips have wanted to minimise the ability of MPs, particularly more independent-minded ones on select committees, to create trouble for the executive, and to delay or substantially amend its plans – though their influence has been much reduced by the 2010 changes to elect committee members. At each stage there have been battles between those stressing the role of the executive/party in power and those stressing the role of Parliament.

Critics of MPs frequently make the error of treating Parliament as if it is a separate – and invariably weak – institution in contrast with an all-powerful government. This represents a profound misunderstanding of Britain's constitutional arrangements. Britain does not have a separation of powers between the executive and legislature as in presidential systems – though some MPs on both the populist right and constitutional reform left have been urging such a separation in order to strengthen the role of Parliament. At present, we have the crown, now the government of the day, in Parliament with ministers sitting in both Houses, deriving their power explicitly from the loyalty of MPs. Party ties come first, and quite naturally, to most members. Most MPs are instinctively tribal and, for the majority of the time, do not have to be corralled by the whips – contrary to the popular but false myths put about on both the left and the right. Whips are seldom cuddly, but they have much less power than in the past. However the twin extremes of absolute loyalty to party and government and an independent Commons versus the executive are both misleading. It is a question of balance, as reflected in the title of a notable report of the Liaison Committee in 2000 entitled 'Shifting the Balance'. MPs have multiple roles and duties: for their parties, for their constituents and as members of the House of Commons.

The overall picture is of a more vigorous and lively Parliament than is commonly assumed. Michael Ryle, a level-headed and reflective former senior clerk of the Commons, concluded in an essay looking back on his long career (Giddings, 2005) that:

Simple factual comparison with the 1950s and early 1960s shows that Parliament – particularly the House of Commons – plays a more active, independent and influential role in Britain today than at any time for many years. Important reforms are still needed, but the major advances in the past fifty years should not be derided. Governments can no longer ignore parliamentary opinion. MPs must be heeded or the media will put goverment in the dock for being out of touch with the public.

CHAPTER SIX

BIG BANG –
CONSTITUTIONAL REFORM

THE ANTI-POLITICIAN MOOD has fuelled demands to put checks on MPs through sweeping constitutional changes. The advocates of big bang reform claim to want to revitalise politics, but, in practice, they are seeking to challenge, and undermine, representative democracy, and hence the role of politicians. Many of the arguments overlap with those in the depoliticisation debate in an earlier chapter. But the direction is different. It is to change the way in which political power is exercised.

The big bang reformers move beyond the personal excesses and abuses of individual politicians to condemn the whole system as rotten and corrupt. They spit out Westminster as a term of insult. They mistrust elected politicians and parties as inherently self-serving and therefore obstacle to the Peoples' (always a capital P) will. There is something of the piety, self-satisfaction and all-or-nothing certainty of a religious cult about them. You are with us in condemning the current system or you are tainted by it.

Their demands are distinct both in scope and in assumptions from the substantial, but essentially gradualist, changes since 1997. It has been common on the right to denounce the changes introduced by the Blair government as amounting to a dismantling of the age-old British constitution. Not only does this ignore the continually evolving nature of our constitutional practices but it also misunderstands the post-1997 legislation.

These changes were undoubtedly substantial – devolution of power in Scotland, Wales and, off and now on, in Northern Ireland; a directly elected mayor in London and some other towns and boroughs; statutory rights to freedom of information; regulation of elections and political parties; removal of most of the hereditary peers from participation of the House of Lords; and, perhaps most important of all, the Human Rights Act. This is leaving aside John Prescott's failed experiment in regional government for England, doomed by the overwhelming defeat of an elected regional assembly for the north-east. And electoral reform for the House of Commons fell by the wayside, at least until the 2010 coalition agreement, following the Blair government's rejection of the Jenkins Committee report of 1999 (even though the first-past-the-post system has been dropped for all the new representative bodies created since 1997, as well as for elections to the European Parliament).

These measures are all consistent with each other, but they do not form part of a coherent overall plan akin, say, to the deliberations of the American founding fathers in Philadelphia in 1787. This is partly because the origins of the push for constitutional reform in 1997 were so diverse, from national interests (Scottish and Welsh), professional interests (lawyers and civil libertarians), and single-issue campaign interests (freedom of information). As Professor Vernon Bogdanor argued (2009):

> The real achievement of constitutional reform is to have redistributed power, but it has redistributed power between elites, not between elites and the people. It has redistributed power 'downwards' to politicians in Edinburgh, Cardiff, Belfast and London, 'sideways', to the life peers in the House of Lords and 'sideways' to the judges interpreting the Human Rights Act.
>
> The value of this dispersal of power should not be underestimated. It has made it easier for the power of government to be made subject to constitutional control...

In that sense, with the crucial exception of the growth of judicial activism symbolised by, but not created by, the Human Rights Act, the effect has not been to challenge representative democracy, but to redefine it.

Looked at another way, these changes have preserved the doctrine of the sovereignty of Parliament. The crown/executive in Parliament is still able to make and unmake laws changing all other aspects of the government system – and hence the traditional powers of politicians are preserved. The Scotland Act of 1998 specifically said that sovereignty remained with Westminster which could, in theory, repeal Scottish devolution. In practice, however, any substantial change in the powers of the Scottish government and Parliament would require the approval of the Scottish people. Similarly, the Human

Rights Act of 1998 did not establish judicial supremacy, the ability to strike down or annul Acts of Parliament. However, the ability of the judges to issues declarations of incompatibility saying that a law or executive decision clashes with the Act has, in practice, operated as a constraint on the executive and the legislature.

Back in 1975, the Wilson government breached the principle of parliamentary supremacy by holding a referendum on whether the UK should stay in the then European Common Market – which voters backed by a two-to-one margin. However, in law, this was only advisory – and Parliament retained the final say. Since then several national referendums have been promised – mainly on European issues from membership of the euro to the original Lisbon treaty on an EU constitution – but none has been held until the one on whether to switch to an Alternative Vote method of electing MPs. Referendums are also proposed as one of the safeguards required to approve any substantial transfer of power from Westminster to Brussels. Otherwise, the main referendums have been at a sub-national level to approve new representative bodies in Scotland, Wales, Northern Ireland and London, and to reject an assembly for north-east England.

But, in general, constitutional reform has not so far redistributed power from the politicians to the voter. That, according to Bogdanor, is its crucial weakness, why it has made so little impact on entrenched attitudes towards the political system. It has not gone far enough in implementing the radical programme of the constitutional reforming liberals of the nineteenth century. There is no evidence that the programme has succeeded in reversing the recent decline in confidence in government or 'reconnecting voters with politicians'.

However, the all-out reformers argue that in view of this deep disillusionment with mainstream politics, and politicians, there is a need for more radical reform to give voters more direct say. On this view, representative democracy, as familiar in Britain for at least 150 years, has outlasted its usefulness. Bogdanor has, therefore, maintained that the next, and a far more difficult, stage of reform must be a redistribution of power from politicians to the people. As I pointed out in Chapter Two, this is one of the aims of the coalition government's 'Big Society' programme, but in this case it is to individuals as principally citizen/consumers rather than as citizen/voters. The 'Big Society' is more about choice than voice. The constitutional reformers are in many cases opposed to the 'Big Society' vision as threatening the break-up of collective provision. Instead, what they want is an end to the era of pure representative democracy, defined by voter involvement largely at general elections and then a largely deferential acceptance of the Burkean view of the MP as representative rather than delegate.

There is a strong case for greater involvement by voters in political decisions affecting them, but not at the cost of undermining effective government. This is the central argument of the book which I will pursue in later chapters in looking at ways of reconciling greater popular participation with a still largely representative democracy. In this chapter, I want to focus on the case for the prosecution. This was made most forcefully in the report of the Power Inquiry in spring 2006. The inquiry (a large-scale enterprise backed by the Joseph Rowntree Charitable Trust and the Joseph Rowntree Reform Trust) argued for sweeping changes in the way we are governed. Its central theme was that there is deep alienation, particularly among the young, from the political system, which amounts to 'a contempt for formal politics in Britain'. The report highlighted a big contrast between the decline in membership of political parties and evidence of a continuing high level of interest both in political issues and in voluntary activism. Accordingly, the report called for a rebalancing of relations between the executive and the legislature, and between central and local government. This includes electoral reform for all tiers of democracy, from local councils to the House of Commons and House of Lords. But the most controversial aspect lay in the recommendations that challenge the basis of representative democracy through a big extension of participatory democracy. The report discusses deliberative procedures such as citizens' juries, forums and the like. The underlying approach is based upon an inherent mistrust of 'the political elite behind closed doors'.

The Power report has been acclaimed by many on the left but sharply criticised by many political scientists for both its analysis and recommendations. There are lots of unsubstantiated assertions and a reluctance to take account of alternative views. Along with other critics, the report highlights the very sharp decline in turnout in the 2001 general election, only partially reversed in the 2005 and 2010 elections. But that decline can be explained more by the absence of competitive elections in 2001 and 2005, as well as disenchantment with the two main parties, which helped boost both the Liberal Democrats and other, smaller parties. There is no clear-cut link between turnout and political disengagement. 'The message of disappointment, frustration and anger with our elected leaders and the institutions of politics' noted by the Power report may have been as much to do with public hostility to an unpopular government, fuelled by discontent over the Iraq

War as with the structures of government. Disillusion may have been, and may still be, more about the performance of government than the processes of how we are governed.

Moreover, it is wrong to suggest that there is a big divorce between supposedly moribund party politics and thriving informal issue-based politics. There is, in practice, a large overlap between those participating in single-issues groups and in formal politics. Contacting representatives and voting remains much higher than taking part in demonstrations and being active in campaigning groups.

Another weakness in the Power Inquiry is the assertion that political disengagement is a response to political structures rather than attitudes towards particular events. There is little evidence from other countries that changes in the way elections are conducted – away from first-past-the-post towards more proportional systems – result in increases in turnout or satisfaction with the political system. Indeed, most Western democracies suffer similar problems of disengagement and low levels of trust as Britain, and virtually all have proportional systems of election and most have federal constitutions with decision-making decentralised to regional and local levels, as the Power report recommends.

Moreover, the Hansard Society's Annual Audit of Political Engagement has contradicted claims that the public wants to participate actively in national decision-making. Declan McHugh, former director of the Parliament and government programme for Hansard and later special adviser to Jack Straw, argued (2006) that, on the basis of the Audit, a majority (68 per cent) wanted to have a say in how the country is run. This was much higher (82 per cent) among professionals and managers than among unskilled workers (53 per cent).

However, further questions suggest that there is a big gap between this broad desire and concrete intentions. Beyond signing petitions (72 per cent), the vast majority of those interviewed were unwilling to take further actions. Those which demand a commitment of time, such as taking part in a governmental or parliamentary consultation, attracted even less support (13 per cent). As McHugh noted, when the Audit went beyond discussing the actions that people were willing to take to influence or protest against a decision, to asking about what actions they had taken, the numbers fell even further. While 26 per cent said they might be willing to attend a demonstration, only 13 per cent had done so, and just 4 per cent had taken part in a consultation. The top activity was signing a petition which just 50 per cent had done.

These conclusions have been confirmed by later Audits, as well as by other surveys. According to the 2011 Audit, the number signing a petition had fallen to a new low of 36 per cent, after rising to 40 per cent in the previous year, still less than in 2006. The number of people who had taken part in three or more activities remained in the mid-teens. The most active were aged between forty-five and sixty-four. And, by a wide margin, were more likely to be middle class than working class. There is ample other evidence of low levels of participation in discussions held by local community partnerships and in elections for NHS Foundation Trusts. As McHugh concluded: 'New methods of direct engagement will fail significantly to increase activism among the overwhelming majority – no matter how frustrated they presently claim to be.' This does not mean that the public is uninterested or does not want to be kept informed. But there is a difference between being heard and wanting to act.

So any attempt to strengthen public participation needs to take account of the danger that only a minority, and probably only a small minority, will be active. As McHugh argued:

While the call for more participatory democracy has a visceral emotional appeal, in practice it may only succeed in engaging those already over-represented among voters and party members – that is, the educated, affluent and middle-aged. Mechanisms designed to provide greater opportunities for citizens to participate more directly in decision-making as a means of increasing legitimacy and reducing the perceived democratic deficit may therefore have the opposite effect.

There is the real risk that, instead of popular participation, we will only see involvement by vocal, and self-selecting, interest groups. I am inherently suspicious when I hear someone speaking on behalf of a local community: who chose them? (Community has become one of those all-purpose words intended to have a positive connotation, like that ghastly term stakeholder, which appears to confer legitimacy but, in reality, muddles understanding. Political correctness, or PC, similarly lacks any precise meaning apart from indicating that the writer or speaker dislikes what he is describing.) How about the interests of those who do not have the time or inclination to be involved in such groups? Whenever the People are invoked, I wonder which People? The vocal and active minority, or the majority? That is why I am sceptical about citizens' juries and deliberative assemblies, groups of voters brought together to consider issues and then to produce a verdict. By definition, the participants do not – cannot – represent anyone but themselves, and much depends on the moderator who guides and leads the debate. These are useful consultative tools, but no more. They are not the way to take decisions.

The growth of the internet has led to claims that active participation no longer requires physical presence in the same place, as in a Greek city state (and that was limited in practice) or an American town hall meeting, but can be achieved through cyberspace. The internet can certainly be a tool both to ensure voters are better informed and to enable them to express their concerns and views. But, again, there is the problem of representativeness, as can be seen in the weird range of comments posted on websites by a strident minority. It is like the phone-in polls liked by tabloid papers and some TV stations in which people telephone in or, now, text their views on an issue of the day. These are completely worthless as measures of public opinion since they only reveal the views of those bothered enough about an issue to take the effort and to incur the cost of expressing their opinions. Such surveys, rightly described as voodoo polls by Bob Worcester, the founder of MORI, are measures of activity, not opinion. None of these mechanisms enables choices to be made on complicated issues where multiple trade-offs and compromises will be required.

Participatory democracy has attractions at a local, neighbourhood level, but not nationally in reconciling conflicting preferences and pressures on public spending, taxation and borrowing. That is a job for politicians elected by, and acting on behalf of, all the people, not a self-selecting minority. That is not an argument for the status quo. There is ample scope to reform representative democracy, to make its institutions more open and to give voters greater opportunities to make their views known, via e-petitions, and even referendums in carefully defined cases – as I will discuss in a later chapter.

The big bang reformers also tend to favour comprehensive changes leading to a codified or written constitution laying down the specific powers of various tiers of institution. By turn, this covers everything from systems of election, the extent of devolution, the role and composition of a second chamber to the power of the judiciary. These are all in themselves important and difficult issues which affect the balance of power. For instance, any move towards a proportional system of election – as in the devolved bodies in the United Kingdom and in the rest of Europe – would mean that one party could probably not win an outright majority in a general election, resulting in either minority governments or coalitions. And as we have seen since May 2010, coalitions imply a different style of politics. Moving towards a federal structure, as in Germany and Spain, would have profound implications for not only the scope of central government but also for taxation and public spending decisions. At present, with the exception of the provisions of the Parliament Acts of 1911 and 1949 affecting finance Bills and any extension in the life of a parliament, relations between the Commons and Lords are determined by convention and precedent. But the creation of a wholly or predominantly elected second chamber – the theoretical position of all three main parties in the Commons (if not of these parties' members of the Lords) – would almost certainly require a revision and formalisation of these arrangements.

Any or all of these changes would lead to a codified or written constitution enacted by Parliament. It is wrong to say that Britain has a wholly unwritten constitution now. Rather, we have a series of statutes, conventions and, increasingly in the past twenty years, codes of various kinds, defining the behaviour of ministers, MPs, civil servants and special advisers. But most are intended to be non-justiciable in the sense that the decision on whether such conventions and codes have been broken lies with politicians. The Prime Minister retains the sole right to determine whether the Ministerial Code has been broken and what should happen to an offender. Similarly, while the Parliamentary Commissioner for Standards, and his more recent counterpart in the Lords, has created an independent investigator of misconduct, ultimate decisions on whether the code has been breached, and what punishment there should be, still lie with MPs and peers. Sir Gus O'Donnell, the Cabinet Secretary, was careful to ensure that the Cabinet Manual, produced in draft in December 2010 to bring together conventions and practice on the working of government, was to provide guidance and was not in any way a step towards a written constitution.

Gordon Brown from time to time raised the prospect of a written or statutory constitution. The Green Paper on constitutional change ('The Governance of Britain'), the first initiative of his premiership in July 2007, expressed the issue in terms of unifying values and national identity. This reflected Brown's concern as a Scottish MP at a time of devolution to provide definitions of Britishness bringing together all parts of the country. The trouble is that this can sound, and often sounded, nebulous, amounting to little more than a belief in the NHS and fairness, underpinned by Brown's understandable desire to justify himself as a UK Prime Minister against some populist anti-Scots prejudice. But such talk said nothing about the nature of governing relationships inherent in a codified or written constitution. The Green Paper underlined the 'need to ensure that Britain remains a cohesive society, confident in its shared identity' and 'to provide a clear articulation of British values'. The conclusion was that 'this might in time lead to concordat between the executive and Parliament or a written constitution'.

But nothing happened. Like much of the rest of Brown's constitutional programme, it slipped down the list of priorities, as a result of the increasing preoccupation with the banking crisis and its aftermath and a lack of drive from the top. Michael Wills, then a Minister at the Justice Department, sought to produce a statement of British values. I attended a seminar in the dining room of 10 Downing Street in spring 2009 with some distinguished political scientists and theorists to discuss the development of a British constitution. But it all seemed vague and far too late, and the debate disappeared before the general election. If the Brown government wanted to make progress on the constitutional front, there were more urgent priorities, such as interim arrangements for the House of Lords. In particular, the Brown government never addressed the fundamental questions underpinning a written or statutory constitution. Until there was agreement on the electoral system, the second chamber and central/devolved and local relations, you could not make a start on writing such a constitution.

The big bang reformers have ignored such preconditions. For the likes of the Unlock Democracy group or the Our Kingdom website, such issues are already settled in their minds and must be self-evident to all who believe in democracy. What Professor Anthony King (2007) has aptly called the constitutional holists have no doubts. For them, a UK-wide constitutional convention must be summoned to draft a formalised written constitution, with a capital C. As Jack Straw, Justice Secretary from 2007 until 2010 pointed out, a fully elected representative body already exists in the form of the House of Commons, but, to the big bang reformers, this is tainted by the vested interests of existing politicians. But it is unclear how a constitutional convention would be different unless it was formed by self-selecting groups of the People, or organisations from civic society, which could not be representative. Professor King poured scorn on such calls, arguing that there was no popular demand for either a convention or a written constitution, nor, crucially, any agreement on what should be included. What is self-evident to the big bang reformers is not obvious to others.

The key element in this debate is the role of the judiciary. As noted above, the supremacy of Parliament is still observed in statute – with the significant exception of European Union law which is superior to UK law if there is a conflict. However, the courts can only act in this way because of the European Communities Act 1972, on UK entry, which could be repealed. This issue has been revived in the controversy over the Bill asserting British sovereignty on European issues. (For the sake of brevity, and despite the entreaties of Bill Cash I can hear even as I write, I will not go down this path, important though it is.) The Human Rights Act confirmed parliamentary supremacy in this way, while the Supreme Court created by the 2005 law which changed the running of the judiciary retained the same powers as the former Law Lords. But this needs to be heavily qualified in practice. Even before the Human Rights Act, there had been a steady growth in judicial activism associated with the increasing use of judicial review against the decisions of the government. Since the passage of the Act, the rulings of the Law Lords/Supreme Court have forced the government to change policy, particularly in terrorism cases.

In parallel, there has been a growing debate about whether a certain class of constitutional laws should be given special treatment and protection. This issue was raised by a number of judges at various stages of the court hearings over the legality of using the 1949 Parliament Act to push through the law to ban hunting with dogs. In this case, Lord Steyn argued that in exceptional circumstances, involving an attempt to abolish judicial review or the ordinary role of the courts, the Law Lords/Supreme Court 'may have to consider whether this is a constitutional fundamental which even a sovereign Parliament acting at the behest of a complaisant House of Commons cannot abolish'. Other senior judges have talked similarly of 'a higher order law' which cannot be repealed like other laws. On this view, the power of a democratically elected government or parliament cannot be absolute: for instance, it could not override the institution of free and regular elections. These judicial statements have partly been in response to what judges have seen as misguided ministerial interventions into the role of the courts as the final arbiters of the interpretation and application of the law.

This debate has produced a strong counter-reaction from politicians, reinforced by the media, not just populist protests against unpopular rulings, but also warnings by lawyer/politicians against judicial activism straying too far into the political arena.

The late Lord Bingham, one of the wisest recent judges on these issues, was more cautious (2010):

The British people have not repelled the extraneous power of the papacy in spiritual matters and the pretensions of royal power in temporal in order to subject themselves to the unchallengeable rulings of unelected judges. A constitution should reflect the will of a clear majority of the people.

He warned, however, that 'the constitutional settlement has become unbalanced, and the power to restrain legislation favoured by a clear majority of the Commons has become much weakened, even if, exceptionally, such legislation were to infringe the rule of law'. So judges should be wary of taking on the role of elected politicians. But it also involves politicians accepting that there are 'some rules which no government should be free to violate without legal restraint'. We are a very long way from having a proper public debate – let alone taking a decision – on whether we want to replace the sovereignty of Parliament by the sovereignty of a codified and entrenched constitution. The outcome will depend on the restraint shown by both politicians and judges.

CHAPTER SEVEN

THE MEDIA – THE FERAL BEAST

POLITICIANS AND THE MEDIA are locked in an embrace of mutual dependency, occasional friendship, frequent suspicion and barely hidden bitterness and scorn. The relationship will always be tense, for good reasons since the interests of seeking power and governing, and exposing and scrutinising, are fundamentally different. But we have moved a long way from the High Victorian talk of the Fourth Estate or the grand assertions of press independence in Delane's *Times*. For many politicians, the media are the enemy, while, for many in the media, the political class is inherently corrupt and weak.

There are two interconnected charges. First, the media are often blamed by politicians, and academics, for the current low standing of Parliament. Newspapers and, to only a slightly lesser extent, broadcasters are depicted as being on an anti-politician crusade, seizing on scandals and, even more, trumped up scandals to undermine representative democracy. On this view, the media show no understanding of the work of politicians, nor of the complexities, compromises and risks involved in government.

There are no shades or subtleties. The tone is wholly critical and negative. In short, as John Lloyd, my old *Financial Times* colleague and now media commentator and academic, has argued (notably in his 2004 polemic *What the Media are Doing to Our Politics*), the media has become an alternative establishment, claiming as much legitimacy as elected representatives and fostering a culture of inherent mistrust of the motives of politicians. At the same time, it ignores the intricacies and complexities of policymaking. Similarly, Professor Matthew Flinders has put the point in what he describes as 'fairly harsh terms' (2010):

> If we really want to understand how the public are mislead, abused and exploited then it is to journalism and the media and not just to politicians and politics, that we should turn ... It is a curious paradox of modern times that just as we have more media space than ever, its content is generally found to have less and less healthy debate.

These concerns have been fuelled by a trio of controversies current at the time of concluding this book: first, the disclosure of secret diplomatic exchanges by Wikileaks; second, the sting operation by the *Daily Telegraph* using undercover reporters against Liberal Democrat ministers; and, third, the allegations of extensive phone hacking by the *News of the World* against leading politicians and celebrities. All three, and particularly the latter two, stories have reinforced politicians' criticisms of the media. All three raise questions of whether it is any longer possible to maintain boundaries of privacy and secrecy in the age of the internet and easily accessible telecommunications.

The second, and related, charge is that the media – and, in particular, the broadcasters – have usurped the function of politicians. The age of deferential relations between supplicant and, generally socially inferior, journalists, and upper class, disdainful politicians is long gone. If anything, the deference is now the other way around. Senior journalists, editors and top politicians have now been educated in the same places, and have often moved across from one world to the other. That can produce excessively cosy relationships, but it has also meant that the media are quite willing, even eager, to assume the role previously exclusively claimed by politicians. The main political debates now occur in their studios and on their terms. This has not only sidelined the House of Commons as the main arena for debate and scrutiny but has also, consequently, distorted representative democracy. On this view, ministers are answerable far more to highly paid celebrity broadcasters and columnists than to MPs elected to hold them to account. Ministers worry far more about a grilling by Jeremy Paxman or John Humphrys than by an appearance in the Commons chamber.

As a journalist for forty years – for roughly three-quarters of the time writing specifically about politics – I have had direct experience of most of these issues and have some sympathy with the charges. The way that the media reports politics is often one-sided. Politicians are treated as inherently on the make, and take. There is no attempt to differentiate between what is in the public interest and what should be entirely private. The coverage of government decisions is too often either narrowly partisan or fails completely to appreciate the hard choices facing ministers. There is too often a blame culture which shows no understanding of the risk calculations faced by any decision-maker. This discourages innovation in the public sector and encourages a safety-first attitude. The *Daily Mail* – or even more ludicrously, the vacuously populist *Daily Express* – is all for cutting the Budget deficit but then opposes any measures hitting the middle-class – as if all the cuts can be made by eliminating waste, dealing with welfare scroungers or slashing international aid. All civil servants are depicted as idle and pampered 'pen pushers'. Yet – and that is why my sympathy for the anti-media charges is limited – some politicians are scoundrels, and, in a few cases, criminals, and more show a contemptuous disregard for the public interest. And many of their nefarious activities would never have been exposed but for the media. Moreover, many politicians deserve criticism for their performance in office, and the media retains a vital role in exposing their weaknesses.

However, despite its frequent shortcomings, much media coverage of big issues remains balanced and informative, much more so than thirty or forty years ago – as well as being better written and better laid out. My first paper, the *Financial Times*, remains essential reading for anyone interested in global economic, political, financial and business developments. At the time of writing this chapter, I looked at the past week's copies of my old paper *The Times* and read in-depth coverage of, for example, the disturbances in Egypt, their causes and background, and of the reorganisation of the NHS, which was as good as any in the past, and probably broader and deeper. The best is still excellent. But too much is mediocre.

Taken as a whole, media coverage of politics, and politicians, is far too negative.

The case for the prosecution was put most forcefully in June 2007 by Tony Blair in a speech organised by the Reuters Institute a fortnight before he left 10 Downing Street (both the speech and commentaries, including by myself, were included in a special issue of *The Political Quarterly* later that year). The speech was widely derided by many in the media at the time given the assiduity with which Blair and his advisers courted Rupert Murdoch and other media moguls over so many years (as vividly recounted in Alastair Campbell's diaries which appeared a few weeks later). His complaints about the media sounded hypocritical given his attempts to set the agenda. If Campbell was not solely responsible for putting the term 'spin' into circulation, he was certainly one of its eager godfathers. But even a sinner repenting can still have interesting things to say.

One of Blair's most telling points was how senior people in almost every walk of life are often overwhelmed by the demands of the media. As he said, 'people don't speak about it because in the main they are afraid to'. Many senior politicians I have known have been terrified of intrusion into their private lives and, even more, their families and children. 'Being done over' by one of the Sunday papers or the tabloids is a horrible experience in which the victim is often helpless to counter unfair and unbalanced charges. Since I have ceased being a full-time journalist, I have been struck by the deeply felt hostility towards much media coverage. Obviously, those in power – whether in Whitehall, or, often even more, in business – want to protect their secrets, and, above all, hide their mistakes. But the hostility, especially to the press, runs much deeper than that.

The Blair speech set out five charges:

First, 'scandal or controversy beats ordinary reporting hands down'. True, but that has always been true to some extent. A juicy resignation has also made the headlines ahead of a select committee report. But this tendency towards highlighting personal scandal and splits has increased as individual incidents are exaggerated and presented as broader systemic failures. There is now much less reporting of process and procedure, and of any but the most immediate and headline-attracting policy stories. Moreover, while big issues are still covered well for a short period when their political sensitivity is highest, secondary questions are now largely ignored. There is the pernicious reaction of a journalist eager – too eager – to get a story into the paper or onto a news bulletin: it is 'too good to check', meaning either that it will be denied, or qualified, and so lose its selling point to news executives.

The competitive pressures from declining sales have led to increased sensationalism at both ends of the market. The justification for intrusive investigation has traditionally been that it is in the public interest. But that has increasingly meant what interests the public rather than what is relevant to the public conduct of politicians. The search for 'scandal or controversy' results in a blurring of ethical standards. The *Daily Telegraph*'s use of undercover reporters to infiltrate the constituency surgeries of Liberal Democrat ministers has challenged the privacy of an MP's relationship with its voters, not to reveal wrongdoing but to provoke indiscretion. I doubt if the reclusive Barclay brothers, the owners of the *Daily Telegraph*, would appreciate the same undercover operation against themselves. Such deception undermines trust and is only justified in the most extreme circumstances. Lionel Barber, my former *Financial Times* colleague in Washington and now the paper's editor, summed up the situation well in his Hugh Cudlipp lecture (2011):

> The *Daily Telegraph*'s decision to dispatch two journalists posing as constituents to interview the Business Secretary Vince Cable falls into a very different category than its earlier scoop on MPs' expenses. The latter story, though acquired for money and deeply damaging to the standing of the Westminster class, clearly met the public interest test; the first did not. It was nothing more than entrapment journalism.

But, as Barber argued, '*The Telegraph*'s conduct, while regrettable, pales by comparison with the phone-hacking scandal which has engulfed Rupert Murdoch and News International' – especially at a time when it was seeking regulatory approval to take full control of BSkyB. What has been so damaging for News International, and the tabloids generally, has not just been the revelations but also the attempt to play them down. The three-year battle by News International to establish that it was just a rogue incident involving a single *News of the World* journalist and one private investigator, both convicted of crimes, broke down in face of further disclosures of phone-hacking by journalists on the paper. This has had a major impact not only on the reputation, and previously unchallenged influence, of News International but also on the inept and passive Press Complaints Commission, the self-regulatory body for the press, and the Metropolitan Police, which has had close links with many tabloid papers and failed to pursue the initial investigation rigorously enough. The story could also have lasting implications for the relationship between the media and politicians. So many prominent politicians are alleged to have had their phones hacked that there will be demands for statutory regulation – in part as a form of delayed revenge for the expenses scandal. The biggest of all the media magnates behaved as if it had enough power and influence to make the scandal go away, but it did not, and over-reached itself, much to the delight of many politicians.

Second, 'attacking motive is far more potent than attacking judgement. It is not enough for someone to make an error. It has to be venal. Conspiratorial.' That has got worse, not just with the disappearance of the previous, often cloying, deference towards political leaders (of the 'what have you got to tell us today?' variety), but as more papers have adopted a populist, anti-politician approach. This has been typified by the indiscriminate use of the term 'sleaze', whether about genuine financial misconduct, or about private behaviour, such as adultery, irrelevant to public life. As discussed in Chapter Two, this is linked with a populist condemnation of politicians as a class.

The Wikileaks story is not just about the multitude of disclosures about US diplomacy, but also about media attitudes to government. The often self-righteous Julian Assange, the founder of Wikileaks, waves the banner of free speech and openness, but this is based on an underlying suspicion of, and contempt for, politicians. Officials, and politicians, work 'in collaborative secrecy to the detriment of the population'. There is no recognition that much international negotiation must be in secret if it is to achieve the desirable ends of reconciling divergent interests to achieve peace and stability.

This generalised assertion is very different from specific revelations of wrongdoing. In the latter case, the public interest can be clearly defined but Wikileaks sets itself up as the arbiter of what should be revealed and whether particular individuals will be put in danger.

Third, 'the fear of missing out means that today's media, more than ever before, hunts in a pack. In these modes it is like a feral beast, just tearing people and reputations to bits, but no one dares miss out.' Again, this is not a new phenomenon. The pack hunted as viciously during the Major years. But, after the 2001 election, there was a 'let's get Blair' campaign by the *Daily Mail* and some journalists, as much on the left as the right. Gordon Brown suffered the same fate for all but the first three months of his premiership. There is a desire to 'achieve a kill' when an allegation emerges against a politician, often a charge irrelevant to performance in office. Self-righteousness rules and politicians and their advisers panic, more often than not forcing a minister out in order to pacify the braying media. That was Peter Mandelson's justified complaint against Tony Blair and Alastair Campbell when he was forced from office for the second time in January 2001.

Pack journalism is partly created by the tendency to follow fashion: someone is either 'in' or 'out' and it is very hard to change that conventional wisdom. That is reinforced by the physical location of the main national political reporters together in crowded rooms of the press gallery at Westminster. These often become friends and colleagues as well as competitors. As Adam Smith observed of meetings of businessmen, when journalists are gathered together, the results are not always in the public interest. This can result in 'group thinking'. Nothing is more depressing than seeing a gaggle of journalists together after a news conference or Commons statement and saying to each other 'what is the story?' or 'what is the line?'. This is partly a defensive, anti-competitive reaction, a desire for a quiet life. It is not just a lack of intellectual self-confidence, or a reluctance to defy the pack and your friends, that inhibits many reporters from taking their own line. It is also their all-too-accurate fear that the news/ night desks will take their lead from the pack and question what their own reporter has filed. Personally, I was fortunate that, when I was a reporter during the 1980s for the *Financial Times*, my judgement was generally accepted by my editors back at the *FT* offices. However, that was much easier for me as a political editor than for more junior journalists (and the *FT* was, and is, much better to its correspondents than other papers, notably the tabloids, where even political editors were, and are, expected to toe the official line). From 1991 onwards, at *The Times*, I was semi-independent, and occasionally semi-detached, as a commentator, once described by my old friend Peter Hennessy as being 'the professor in the attic'. I saw my job as putting events into context, and into historical perspective, which could appear, and was sometimes intended to be, contrary to the prevailing line of the day.

The general herd instinct is little to do with the now largely defunct lobby system, a confusing term covering both the twice daily briefings by the 10 Downing Street spokesman when Parliament is sitting, and the conventions affecting conversations between journalists and MPs. In the early 1980s, when I became political editor of the *Financial Times*, there was a quasi – and in some cases actual – Masonic culture, with totally unattributable briefings. But this has long ago disappeared – thank heavens.

Everything is now more open and explicit, mainly as a result of the arrival of 24-hour news and a new, younger, generation of political reporters in the 1980s and 1990s (now all well into middle age), reinforced in the past decade by the spread of the internet. Of course, there are still unattributable conversations, but these exist in all forms of journalism, and of life, and many of the key insights into what political leaders are thinking, planning and plotting would not emerge in any other way. At worst, this can lead to lazy and misleading journalism, when a reporter disguises his or her lack of sources by referring to a senior minister or senior backbencher when the story may be based on no more than a brief chat with a special adviser or a new MP spreading gossip. Worst of all are phrases like 'a friend of', generally the minister himself or herself, or 'a Tory grandee' of anyone who has been an MP for more than five years or who is clearly not working-class by origin.

Fourth, 'rather than just report news, even if sensational or controversial, the new technique is commentary on the news being as, if not more, important than the news itself'. This is increasingly true, not least because of the tendency to do stories on speeches or policy announcements before they have happened, and then little or nothing when they have been delivered, apart from commentary on their significance. So the reader or listener has to become an interpreter of preview stories, often, later, searching in vain for the details of what is proposed.

This was a particular trait of the Blair/Brown years, though the practice has continued during the Cameron era. The media advisers, or 'spinners', brief a few favoured journalists about a new initiative in order to set the agenda with their own interpretation.

The speech or announcement then becomes an anti-climax, so editors look just for commentary on the news, rather than the news itself. This applies particularly on television where there is an instinctive preference for 'two-ways', exchanges between a news reader, or anchor as they prefer to be known, in the main studio and a political editor or correspondent outside 10 Downing Street or on College Green with the Palace of Westminster as a backdrop. These 'two-ways' often squeeze out, or replace, straight reports on the event, giving more prominence to commentary than reporting.

Fifth, 'the confusion of news and commentary. Comment is a perfectly respectable part of journalism. But it is supposed to be separate. Opinion and fact should be clearly divisible.' The lines have been increasingly blurred. This is nothing new in the tabloids: the *Daily Express* and the *Daily Mirror* in their heydays half a century ago were hardly unbiased in their treatment of political issues. News stories with attitude have been around for some time, but the 'viewspaper', as *The Independent* has styled itself, is now more the norm rather than exception, not just in the tabloids but in many of what used to be called the broadsheets.

Of course, the selection of stories reflects the priorities of a particular news outlet, reflecting not only its political preferences but also its assessment of what will appeal most to its readers/viewers, both current and those it wants to attract. As someone who used to write a regular commentary, I believe the division between news and commentary should be easy to define.

Blair concluded that 'the final consequence of all this is that it is rare today to find balance in the media. Things, people, issues, stories are all black and white. Life's usual greys are almost entirely absent.' This is an exaggeration. While views are supplanting news – and coverage is increasingly focused on a few big stories, it is still possible to find balance, nuance and subtlety in both news stories and among commentators. They may be rarer than in the past, but they can be found. Overall, if some of the Blair claims stand up, uncomfortably so for someone who spent his career as a journalist, many of the charges are exaggerated, pre-date his arrival in 10 Downing Street and could have been made as forcefully during the Major years. That is perhaps scant comfort. But all occupants of Downing Street tend, by the end of their premierships, and usually much earlier, to feel that the media are uniquely against them. In reality, many of the complaints are the inevitable by-product of a vigorous and challenging press questioning the actions of the executive.

Nonetheless, and this is the second, and most telling, charge, the media is accused of usurping the role of politicians. I will not repeat here the largely familiar story of how reporting of what is said in the chamber of the House of Commons has now largely disappeared from all newspapers (for more detail see my chapter in Riddell, 1998). However, voters can follow exchanges on the already good, and steadily improving, Parliament website, where they can read transcripts of what is said after a delay of only three hours. In that sense, the workings of Parliament are more widely accessible than in the past – but not through the mainstream media.

The battle to ensure that political debate was largely on the politicians' terms was lost back in the mid-1950s with the suspension, then abandonment, of the wartime fourteen-day rule, which banned the discussion of issues on radio and television that were due to come before either chamber over the following fortnight. That was the last hurrah of the age of parliamentary dominance of debate and of deferential journalism. As the ageing Sir Winston Churchill complained at the end of his final premiership, when he was never interviewed on either radio or television: 'It would be shocking to have debates in this House forestalled, time after time, by expressions of opinion by persons who had not the status or responsibility of MPs on this new robot organisation of television and BBC broadcasting.'

The marginalisation of the Parliament as the main forum for debate – except when there are close votes on major issues such as the Iraq War, or, more recently, tuition fees – has been accompanied by an assertion by media leaders of their right to set the terms of the debate. During the first half-dozen years of the Blair premiership, when the Tories were still struggling to rebuild themselves after the rout of 1997, you heard journalists and broadcasters, notably those associated with the *Daily Mail*, claim that the media had become the only effective opposition to the government, with a right and duty to scrutinise and challenge. Yet, again, there is nothing new in fears about excessive media influence. Look back to the futile attempts of the press barons to oust Baldwin from the Conservative leadership eighty years ago, prompting his famous denunciation (partly written by his cousin Rudyard Kipling):

The papers conducted by Lord Rothermere and Lord Beaverbrook are not newspapers in the ordinary acceptance of the term. They are engines of propaganda, for the constantly changing policies, desires, personal wishes, personal likes and dislikes of two men ... What the proprietorship of these papers is aiming at is power, and power without responsibility – the prerogative of the harlot throughout the ages.

More than 150 years ago, Anthony Trollope wrote in *The Warden*, the first of his Barchester novels, about Tom Towers, a thinly disguised portrait/caricature of John Thadeus Delane, editor of *The Times* from 1841 until 1877, at the height of its influence and dominance of the national press. Towers loved

> to listen to the loud chattering of politicians and to think how they were all in his power – how he could smite the loudest of them, were it worth his while to raise his pen for such a purpose. He loved to watch the great men of whom he daily wrote and flatter himself that he was greater than any of them.

But Delane was always a journalist first and foremost. He was certainly close to the leading politicians of his day, notably Palmerston and Aberdeen, but he did not seek to displace them. He dedicated *The Times* of his day to the provision of the most up-to-date information, even if it meant causing annoyance and complaints round the courts and chancelleries of Europe. This included extensive reports of what politicians said in Parliament.

The main change over the past thirty or forty years has been in the balance of the relationship – with the media, big-name journalists as much as owner or editors, seeking to supplant politicians as wielders of power. The closer social links between the media and political classes have worked against the interests of politicians.

In particular, there has been a big rise in the number, and prominence, of commentators, often seeking to set the terms of the public debate. Fifty years ago, there were barely a handful of columnists: most opinion was expressed through anonymous leaders. But, now, every paper has a stable of twenty or more columnists, who have become the prized stars of their papers, earning more money than leading news reporters, but also, increasingly, taking their space. Moreover, it is not just the number of columnists but also their style. In the past decade, we have seen the rise of the ranters, the columnists with little knowledge but strong opinions. They have tended to eclipse the more considered analytical columnists, who base their opinions on insider information and insights. The leading examples from the mid-1970s onwards were David Watt, Peter Jenkins and Hugo Young, all of whom died in their prime, Young being the last in 2003. All three, whom I knew and respected, had a distinctive viewpoint, from the liberal centre to the centre-left, hostile to the extremes of both left and right, and could be criticised as being part of the liberal establishment. But, crucially, they saw their prime role as informing and stimulating rather than haranguing. They were engaged in a debate not an argument. This approach has survived in a few columns, but has increasingly been eclipsed by columnists who put opinion ahead of information. We have had the rise of the all-purpose commentators, denouncing all and sundry and ever ready to express an opinion on any subject, regardless of whether they have any expertise about it. At the top end, there is the ubiquitous military historian Max Hastings, while, further down-market, the *Daily Mail* has a stable of writers able to lament some new development, often based on the flimsiest of evidence, in what are known as 'why-oh-why' articles. And that is leaving aside the ranters of the red-top tabloids.

The shift away from informing to provoking has been linked to the importation of the American phenomenon of the committed columnist, which originated in the highly partisan editorial pages of *The Wall Street Journal*. The polarisation of American politics from the Clinton era onwards, through the Bush years to the Obama presidency has resulted in the rise of the ideologically committed op-ed writer. The highly partisan, 'for us or against us', style of writing is not only predictable but is also not really journalism. It seeks to argue on behalf of particular interests rather than explain on behalf of the general reader. That is partly a reflection of the crossover from politics to journalism, and of the desire of many to keep a foot in both camps, to be players (as advisers to leading politicians) as well as journalists. Some can be excellent and thought-provoking columnists. But there is always a doubt about where their true loyalty lies: whether something is being held back in order not to annoy political allies. In the USA, the likes of Glenn Beck of Fox News, on the right, and Jon Stewart, the liberal comedian, have become major political figures, not just through the 'shock jock' style of their programmes intended to arouse their audiences to anger rather than understanding but also in organising rival rallies in August and October 2010 before the mid-term elections. As John Lloyd noted (2011), the effect has been to reduce government by comparison.

> The implicit message, especially from Beck, is that governance is a simple matter of political will. Once this is in place, reform can be achieved with ease. In this environment, journalism becomes a high decibel slate

of complaint of tenuous assertion ... Its protagonists constantly assert that it is a way of holding power to account, and, therefore, in the public interest. There is no question that these rival polemics have stirred up much public interest. But as representative politics is itself represented as a betrayal of a free people, politicians in the centre must worry that they are being displaced not just in rhetoric but in function.

Politicians have increasingly seen themselves as the weaker half of the relationship, and have assiduously courted owners, editors and even ordinary journalists. Over three decades, I attended many breakfasts, lunches and even the occasional dinner between the editor and senior executives of the paper for whom I was working and the Prime Minister of the day, or another senior minister or party leaders. There was always mutual flattery, interest in the paper's leaders and in each other's opinions. I have never ceased to wonder why anyone is interested in the leader line of a paper, particular a broadsheet, which influences few voters. Leaders do not really represent the views of a paper collectively or its readers, but rather those of the editor and half a dozen leader writers. I was a part-time leader writer for a year on *The Times* and found it boring, artificial and formulaic. No matter, Prime Ministers flatter editors by rehearsing the arguments of recent leaders.

Much, much worse are the dinners and receptions held at party conferences when not only editors but also senior executives descend to wine and dine leading politicians. There is a competition about which paper can invite the most big names. This created a tiresome chore in the late summer for my old colleague Philip Webster, when he was political editor of *The Times*, which he always successfully handled, calling in some old favours from longstanding contacts. The dinners, invariably at an over-priced restaurant, could be fun if the great ones were not there, but they could be gruesome if they were. I remember one in Manchester in 2008 with a senior member of the Brown Cabinet and James Murdoch, chairman of News International. The younger Murdoch has little of the instinctive feel, and affection, for newspapers which his father has, and is perhaps rightly more interested in new media developments. He also has little of the buccaneering charm of his father, and his views, of the conventional low tax/deregulatory corporate kind, would be of little interest but for his position and his name. His opinions were treated with awkward politeness by the senior minister, and fawning approval by the News International executives present. It was a bit like humouring a junior member of the Royal Family.

Rupert Murdoch himself is rightly acclaimed as one of the most original media forces of the past half century, with more on the positive side of the ledger than his critics acknowledge. His successful challenge to the printing unions at Wapping in 1986 enabled many of his newspaper rivals to survive, rather than go under, while Sky has vastly improved the coverage of many sports. Murdoch has also been a risk taker, most recently over charging for online content. There are big downsides too, partly as a result of his very success in becoming such a major player. He has acquiesced in a stridency, vulgarity and intrusiveness into private lives which has lowered media standards, though News International has hardly been alone in this. Richard Desmond's tacky products have been far worse.

During my nineteen years on *The Times*, as a semi-detached columnist and commentator, I was never instructed to take a particular line or approach to any opinion piece or analysis – though I was asked to write about some subjects seen as more topical than others, a perfectly reasonable editorial prerogative. Successive editors of *The Times* have adopted a pluralist approach to the views expressed on the op-ed pages, as shown during the Iraq War when two of the most prominent columnists, Matthew Parris and Simon Jenkins, were strong opponents of the military action, which was vigorously supported in the paper's leader columns. Such diversity would not have been tolerated in, say, *The Sun*. However, *The Times* tends to defend, and occasionally promote, the broader commercial and business interests of the News International group on issues of regulation and the like.

Over this period, I had little direct contact with the proprietor as he was often known. On my few meetings with Rupert Murdoch, I found him amusing and shrewd, with a strong dislike of the British establishment, like his own father, and imbued in the values of American big business. His suspicion of Europe seemed more to do with dislike of Brussels regulations than with any alleged threat to British sovereignty. His influence over day-to-day life on *The Times* was limited for those below the top executive level. This was hardly surprising given the size of the News Corporation empire around the world. But he has been much more closely involved on a day-to-day basis with *The Sun*, whose political journalists have looked to his lead. His main influence over *The Times* has been over the choice of editors and over budgets – and hence pricing and design innovations – and hardly at all on day-to-day editorial decisions. The most notable sign of his power has come on his regular three-monthly visits to London when the top editorial team becomes almost wholly preoccupied with his whims and views. The occupational health risk at Wapping for senior executives is crick-in-the-neck from looking up to detect the wishes of the Sun King in the court-like atmosphere which he has successfully cultivated to assure his power over his subordinates.

The wooing of Rupert Murdoch by New Labour has been well-documented, not least in Alastair Campbell's diaries (2007, 2010 and 2011). Campbell and Labour leaders believed – wrongly – that *The Sun*'s personal attacks on Neil Kinnock in the 1992 election had cost the party victory then, and they were determined to neutralise its influence. Tony Blair does not spend much time in his memoirs (2010) discussing his relationship with Rupert Murdoch, though he does at least mention his influence, unlike Margaret Thatcher in her autobiography. Blair writes about the outrage in the Labour Party and among close allies when he accepted an invitation to address the News Corporation conference in Australia in July 1995: 'Now, it seems obvious: the country's most powerful newspaper proprietor, whose publications have hitherto been rancorous in their opposition to the Labour Party, invites us into the lion's den. You go, don't you?' His visit led later to the endorsement of New Labour, or rather Blair, by *The Sun* on the eve of the 1997 general election. But, in reality, *The Sun* was following, rather than leading, its readers. MORI, the then pollsters for *The Times*, used to break down political support by newspaper readership. This showed that *Sun* readers had already deserted the fractious Tory party in large numbers well before the 1997 election and had shifted behind New Labour. Indeed, the first poll after *The Sun*'s endorsement showed a fractional, and statistically insignificant, swing back to the Tories among the paper's readers. I pointed this out to the shrewd and amiable Trevor Kavanagh, its political editor, who always liked to speak on behalf of *Sun*'s readers as a whole as if they were the British People, adding mischievously, 'so much for *The Sun*'s influence?' He was not amused.

The real influence of tabloids and middle market papers has been much less on voting intentions than on underlying attitudes on issues. The relentless euroscepticism, often veering into europhobia, of *The Sun*, the *Daily Mail* and the *Daily Telegraph*, let alone the strident papers in Richard Desmond's stable, did reinforce and strengthen the euroscepticism of the British public. The blame culture of many papers – the invariable calls that 'something must be done' whenever anything goes wrong – has made ministers more risk averse since they know the barrage of criticism they will face if anything goes wrong. The failure to adopt a measured approach to risk is one of the most serious charges against the media at present.

What matters is not just where, and how far, newspapers exercise influence, but, even more, the belief of politicians that they do have such influence. Blair and Campbell treated Murdoch and other proprietors as if they were powerful. On his visits to London, Rupert Murdoch invariably had meetings with Blair, and, increasingly, with Gordon Brown, who was keen to secure his support ahead of his succession to the premiership. It was as if Murdoch was deigning to meet the two most senior ministers in Britain and giving them the benefit of his view, rather than the other way round. Politicians have not been naive in their humouring of Murdoch. Brown also courted Paul Dacre, the long-serving editor of the *Daily Mail*, also to ensure his support for when he became leader. The closeness of Blair and Brown to Murdoch and his editors can give a false impression as to his real influence. The reason why sterling did not enter the euro, fortunately as it turns out, was Brown's opposition, from the devising of the five tests in October 1997 onwards, not the euroscepticism of Murdoch and *The Sun*. However, the explicit warnings by *The Sun* of its strong opposition to any integrationist moves was undoubtedly an important factor restraining Blair from any bold initiatives on Europe.

In many ways, the closeness between political leaders and media owners, and editors, is demeaning. The relationships, born of necessity, reek of insincerity. That was shown when *The Sun* brutally dumped Brown and shifted behind David Cameron in the middle of the Labour conference in September 2009. And, like 1997, it probably made little difference given the earlier shift against Brown and Labour of many *Sun* readers.

As Lance Price, a former BBC reporter and Downing Street spinner under Campbell, argues (2010) in his thoughtful book on the relationship between Prime Ministers and the media:

It is a consistent feature of the long battle for supremacy between Downing Street and the media that those prime ministers who fretted most about getting the support of the media not only failed to keep it, but also performed less well in office as a consequence of trying ... In their different ways, and in the face of very different challenges, the prime ministers of the past hundred years who had the greatest impact were also those who fretted least about the media: Margaret Thatcher because she didn't need to, Winston Churchill because he had more important things to do, and Clement Attlee because he simply wasn't interested.

At one level, it is much harder nowadays to keep a distance from the media – when Prime Ministers and political leaders are being urged from all sides to find someone who can manage the press and broadcasters, a new Alastair Campbell. Such heads of communication, no longer just spokesmen, are now major figures themselves in a way that Francis Williams (working for Attlee) or Harold Evans (for Eden and Macmillan) never were. (Evans was not, of course, the same as the later *Sunday Times* editor and journalistic sage.)

Yet, paradoxically, the politicians' concern with courting media magnates has intensified just at a time when the mainstream media are struggling for financial survival. The decline in sales of newspapers, even the most successful ones, has been stark. The UK newspaper market has shrunk by more than a fifth since 2004, with both broadsheets and tabloids being badly hit. Over the past decade, sales of the *Daily Mirror* have halved, with *The Sun* down by nearly a quarter and even the leading broadsheets (The *Daily Telegraph*, *The Times* and *The Guardian*) falling by between a third and two-fifths. The decline in sales has been compounded by a squeeze on advertising revenues. The main BBC and ITV news bulletins used to have audiences of 8, even 10, million. The average is now well under half that, despite the growth in population. Even in 1995 well over 200 television shows had audiences of more than 15 million; now almost none do. That reflects the explosive growth in the number of television outlets and the ability to watch any programme when you want to do so, through time shifting and DVDs etc. And then there is the internet with the vast number of sites, blogs and social networking forums of all kinds – some of the most successful of which are run by mainstream media organisations such as the BBC and *The Guardian*.

Until the late 1980s, there was a national conversation with a substantial proportion of adults watching the same programmes, listening to the same politicians, at the same time. That world has gone, making it harder for politicians to get their messages across but, in the process, exposing the pretentions of the traditional media whose reach is declining. The change in the media world offers an opportunity to politicians to talk to – and, equally important, listen to – the public.

CHAPTER EIGHT

THE VERDICT

WE NEED POLITICIANS. Much though we may wring our hands over the foibles and misdemeanours of the current bunch of ministers and MPs, we cannot wish them away. Throw the rascals out is always an appealing slogan – and the ability to get rid of one lot of politicians at a general election is the central pre-condition for a healthy and stable democracy. But, then, in come another lot of rascals.

As Hilaire Belloc memorably wrote in his poem 'On a General Election':

> *The accursed power which stands on Privilege*
> *(And goes with Women, and Champagne and Bridge)*
> *Broke – and Democracy resumed her reign*
> *(Which goes with Bridge, and Women and Champagne).*

Substitute sleaze, spin and expenses, and you have probably got a fair view of how most voters view the change in power after an election. It is tempting to shrug your shoulders and say it was always so. Politicians have never been popular or trusted – and there is little that can be done about it.

But such a world-weary shrug will no longer do. The challenges which I have outlined over the previous six chapters – the populist contempt, the excessive partisanship, the unrealistic expectations as well as the self-destructive conduct of some politicians – are not only serious in themselves, albeit often exaggerated, but they are, cumulatively, worse than in the past. Crucially, the current low standing of politicians means that representative democracy does not – and cannot – work as it should. Not only is government made harder, but the anti-politician mood has encouraged the search for alternative approaches which threaten to undermine representative democracy.

Temperamentally, I dislike talk of a crisis in democracy – such extreme language can be left to the ranters. But there is unquestionably something unhealthy about the widespread denigration of politicians. Of course, as I have argued earlier, politicians, in part, have only themselves to blame, not only because of the expenses scandal but also because of a style of politics which invites cynicism and disillusion. The term spin is much over-used: politicians' attempts to set, and manipulate, the media agenda did not start in 1994 when Alastair Campbell began working for Tony Blair. Politicians are regarded as dishonest, not only financially but also in not telling the truth and in raising false expectations. None of this is new. The Marconi scandal of a century ago, which implicated both the Chancellor of the Exchequer and the Attorney-General, was as bad as most recent 'sleaze' scandals, and the sale of honours after the First World War was far worse a century ago than recently. But a more assertive, and often strident, media, amplified by the internet and blogging, have increased both the spotlight on politicians and the level of criticism, and abuse, they face.

These charges against politicians – exaggerated though I regard many of them to be – make it harder for ministers and MPs to operate. If you are widely held in contempt, it is much more difficult for you to engage the sympathy and support of your voters for both the compromises and risks which decisions by government involve.

At root, as many of the academic commentators have pointed out, this fosters false expectations about what politicians – and representative democracy – can achieve. Gerry Stoker (2006) has made the point that 'somehow or other we have forgotten what politics is capable of doing – and, perhaps more importantly, we are unclear about what it can't do. At its most extreme you could argue that the malaise afflicting democratic governance today is many citizens rather wish that they could do without politics.'

Increases in populism and partisanship have resulted in a rejection of many of the underlying assumptions of representative politics: that compromise is to be prized, not condemned, and that your opponents have a legitimate right to their say, and to govern if they win an open and free election. These assumptions have been questioned in the past, notably in the troubled years running up to 1914 when some leading Unionist politicians considered undemocratic means to stop the Irish Home Rule legislation of the Asquith government. We are not in nearly as bad a position as that. But many in the blogosphere reject the legitimacy of political opponents. The assumptions are in absolute terms: either politicians deliver everything we want or they are betraying us.

As serious, the mistrust of politicians has resulted in attempts to take the politics out of certain decisions. In part, as I discussed in Chapter Four, this is ideological, reflecting a belief that ministers and civil servants are the wrong people to be responsible for reaching decisions in some areas. On this view, these activities should be turned over to the private sector through privatisation and the increased use of markets. The coalition government's Big Society agenda has a similar thrust in trying to make individual citizens, or local groups, the main drivers for improved standards in services – rather than politicians. This is partly the age-old debate about the balance between the public and private sectors, but has, increasingly, also reflected a desire to minimise the involvement of politicians.

The main perpetrators of depoliticisation have been politicians themselves. There has been a loss of confidence, even of nerve, in face of all the criticism. Politicians have been on the defensive, complaining about not being understood. At times, they have been ashamed to say that a decision is political: that is reflects a particular series of values, attitudes and interests not shared by everyone and often vigorously opposed by other politicians. Instead, they increasingly want to present issues in a non-political way. This has been seen both in the appointment of outsiders as ministers and advisers and in the desire to legitimise decisions by delegating them to non-political bodies, such as the Monetary Policy Committee or the Competition Commission. There is a strong case for this course in some cases like the MPC, provided those responsible are held fully accountable by Parliament for their actions, as the Bank Governor is by the Treasury Committee. Yet one reason for such moves is the implicit assumption that politicians cannot be trusted to handle crucial decisions as setting interest rates in an economically responsible manner since that they will always put electoral factors first. Hence, we need to be protected from the consequences of politicians.

The danger is that delegating responsibility for regulatory and ethical decisions to impartial bodies is taken too far and extends into areas which are inherently political – such as fixing levels of taxation and public spending. Independent experts, such as the Office for Budget Responsibility, can monitor trends, make forecasts and warn if fiscal policy looks like missing its deficit reduction target, but it is for politicians themselves to fix those targets and decide how they should be achieved. Similarly, there has been repeated talk over the years of taking the NHS out of politics. Of course, clinical decisions should be left to doctors and nurses. But decisions on methods of funding and on the allocation of resources must be taken by politicians since it is only they who are directly answerable to the public.

The constitutional reform programme of the past decade and a half has also been inspired in part by a mistrust of politicians. Some of the measures have been about shifting power from one level of politicians to another. But others – such as the Freedom of Information Act, the creation of the Electoral Commission and the associated legislation – originate in suspicions about the behaviour of politicians, either in preventing the disclosure of secrets or alleged misconduct in fund-raising. This has been part of a general codification of public life, epitomised by the creation of the Committee on Standards in Public Life in 1994, and the consequent rules affecting parliamentarians, civil servants and others in public life. All are motivated by a desire to reduce the previous freedom and discretion of politicians for example, regulating how ministers handle public appointments. The underlying cause of the dissatisfaction of many MPs, and some senior officers of the Commons, with the Independent Parliamentary Standards Authority is not just about the application of tighter rules on their expenses, but is also about an outside body regulating a key aspect of their affairs.

The trickiest area is the boundary between politicians and the judiciary. The growth of judicial review and a human rights culture is rooted in a suspicion of the state, and hence of politicians. It is absolutely correct that the citizen should be protected against arbitrary, unreasonable and disproportionate actions by the state. Similarly people should have legal protection, and recourse to the courts, in defence of fundamental human rights and freedoms, as laid down in the European Convention on Human Rights. When some on the Tory right argue for repeal of the Human Rights Act and its replacement by a British Bill of Rights, it is not clear what rights they would repeal. Their main objection is to the interpretation of the Act in the courts, both in the UK over the past decade and, ultimately, at Strasbourg.

The judges exist to enforce the rule of law and that often involves protecting the rights of unpopular groups such as immigrants and even those convicted of crimes in prison. At present, the British government has accepted – often with reluctance – rulings by the European Court of Human Rights (linked to the Council of Europe, not the European Union), as, so far, it has always changed policy in response to declarations of incompatibility made by UK courts under the Human Rights Act. Critics argue that the European Court has used the Human Rights Act to extend its remit into areas which should properly remain under the control of elected politicians. In short, what are fundamental freedoms and where should politicians still have the final say? That question has arisen over the European Court's ruling – against the strong opposition of both the past and current British governments – that convicted prisoners should have the right to vote. That ruling has infuriated many MPs who regard it as an intrusion into matters which should be properly determined by the British Parliament – and on that, at least, they have the support of a big majority of voters. The objectors argue that, while convicted prisoners should obviously retain fundamental rights – to appeal and against torture, and cruel, inhuman and degrading treatment – the loss of the right to vote is, like the loss of their liberty, part of the price they should pay for being convicted of a crime and being imprisoned. Are all rights of equal standing? But many civil libertarians and lawyers argue that, in all cases, rights and the rule of law as interpreted by the judges should prevail. Cases such as this test the boundary between elected politicians and the judiciary, and human rights law.

This issue of the proper frontier between the expression of the popular will through elected politicians and the rule of law, as interpreted by judges, would arise even more with a formal codified or written constitution. Such a constitution would give judges the power to decide whether legislation passed by Parliament was compatible with the constitution. This is not a narrow matter of laws affecting how we are governed, the electoral system, and relations between the centre and devolved bodies and local authorities. As the US experience shows, the Supreme Court has often taken a highly political interpretation of the remit of the constitution on issues ranging from abortion to limits on election campaign spending.

Consequently, the current criticism of politicians is much more than a populist and media-driven reaction to the alleged, and often exaggerated, misbehaviour of the current crop of MPs and peers. It is about the role of politicians as such: the framework in which they operate and their role in democracy.

So I return to the case for representative democracy, and hence for politicians elected to represent us. There will always be arguments about what should be done by the state and what should remain in the private sector. That is the stuff of political debate. These decisions will, for most of the time, have to be taken by representative bodies. The 'most of the time' caveat would not have been necessary fifty years ago. Then, it was accepted that Parliament should take key decisions on its own on the basis of the election of MPs at least every five years. MPs would listen to outside interests and constituents, but the latter would not have any rights to determine what happened apart from occasionally in the ballot box in choosing MPs. That view has been qualified by the use, and even more the promise, of referendums on important constitutional issues. Such referendums remain, in theory, advisory, but in practice they qualify parliamentary sovereignty. Just think about repealing or significantly amending the Scotland Act of 1998, which created or re-created the Holyrood Parliament, without a referendum of the Scottish people. It is unthinkable. In day-to-day practice, too, MPs consult their constituents, and are bombarded by emails from them, in ways unimaginable in the past.

Nonetheless, with these important caveats, the day-to-day business of government is conducted by a Prime Minister and ministers who can command the confidence of the House of Commons, chosen to represent the public. However much use is made of focus groups, or deliberate forums, like citizens' juries, to test out public views, the only way that differing interests and opinions can be reconciled is by a body elected to represent the public. The legislature in turn holds to account an executive, whose membership is determined by the results of an election. Government by town meeting is unworkable above the level of a local neighbourhood. Even in the age of the internet and interactive television, the government cannot be run by the people, as opposed to on behalf of the people.

Throughout this book I have treated the case for representative democracy and for politicians as synonymous. Some critics would disagree and argue that MPs should be genuine independents, rather than committed politicians, and not have ties to any group. Some would go even further and argue that representatives should be chosen by lot. That is naive nonsense and would be a recipe for anarchy, playing into the hands of those who would remain permanently at the centre, the civil service. Being a minister or an MP requires skills – of communication, of comprehension of issues and of leadership – which have to be developed and cannot be picked up instantly.

One undercurrent of the anti-politician mood is a dislike of political parties. They are seen as reinforcing the inherent flaws in politicians. The argument goes that if MPs were truly independent – as they are completely falsely said to have been in the past – then they could speak unchecked on behalf of their constituents. The result would, however, be confusion and lack of any direction in government. The current major parties are unquestionably flawed, as shown by the fall in their total memberships to barely 2 per cent of the electorate at most. But parties are essential to clarify the choices available to voters and to ensure that policies can be carried through. A House of Commons full of independents would make government impossible since there would be shifting, and wholly unpredictable, majorities from issue to issue and from day to day. Decisions would be even more subject to populist and media-driven pressures than now, That does not address the concern that parties elected on the basis of putting forward one set of ideas in a manifesto then change their minds when in office. This question has been given added force by the creation of the coalition in May 2010 when both Conservatives and Liberal Democrats have had to drop some of their manifesto commitments and agree compromises in the coalition agreement. But that is because neither party on its own gained a majority of votes. This experience also suggests that parties should be more cautious in their election promises.

There are no magic solutions to the current malaise of representative democracy. As Tony Wright, the former Labour MP, has rightly pointed out (2009), many of the problems are cultural as much as structural. They are about the attitudes and behaviour of MPs, peers, the media and, also, the public. In part, they involve recognising we – voters as much as parties – cannot and should not get as much as we want. It is good that we have to recognise the other person's point of view and compromise.

There are many ways in which representative democracy can be made to work better. But I do not believe that they necessarily require, or would even be helped, by 'big bang' constitutional reform. Devising new institutions or mechanisms in addition to existing ones will not make voters any warmer towards politicians. There was a strong case for many of the constitutional reforms introduced since 1997, even if not necessarily in the exact forms they were introduced. Scottish, Welsh and Northern Ireland devolution, and the elected mayors for London and some other towns, have been desirable in themselves, and for the balance of democracy within the United Kingdom. But they have not had any impact on voters' attitudes towards politicians. Politicians in the devolved bodies have faced as much criticism, and of the same kind, as MPs and peers, while voter turnout has remained pretty low in the four yearly elections for these bodies.

Nor is there any evidence from other Western democracies that voters are more favourably inclined towards politicians as a result of adopting a proportional system of elections, having a federal structure with strengthened regional and local government, an elected second chamber and a codified, and justiciable constitution – even though all are regarded as self-evidently correct and necessary by the 'big bang' reformers. There may or may not be a case for some of these changes, and for others, such as having fixed-term parliaments, but they should not be regarded as an answer to the problems of representative democracy. Such changes need to be examined on their own merits, not as part of some alleged and, in practice illusory, grand plan to solve the ills of British democracy.

At this point in most analyses, there is usually high-minded anguish about a loss of trust and a debate about whether, and how, it can be rebuilt. I wrote plenty about this subject during my years as a journalist. But I am now convinced that we are no more likely to convince voters to trust politicians than we are to find the Holy Grail. We return to the conundrum running through this book that reduced deference has both fostered demands for increased transparency and, through increased disclosure, damaged, rather than enhanced, the reputation of politicians.

Many of the changes introduced since the 1990s – notably those associated with the Committee on Standards in Public Life – have been aimed at rebuilding trust. We have had a whole range of initiatives to help restore the reputation of politicians and others in public life: the creation of new regulatory bodies and increased openness on MPs' outside interests and expenses. Most are desirable in themselves, but they have done nothing to increase the public's trust in politicians. Indeed, some changes may have increased voter dissatisfaction. The classic example is Freedom of Information legislation, which, unlike Tony Blair, I do not regret. It was only thanks to the legislation that MPs' expenses were eventually published. However, the consequent revelations about MPs' use, and abuse, of the previous lax system has done more to damage the standing of politicians than anything else. That underlines how welcome measures like FOI can, at least in the short-term, make the position worse.

Onora O'Neill was prescient in her 2002 Reith lectures in warning that some of the regimes of accountability and transparency developed across the previous fifteen years may damage rather than reinforce trustworthiness. Baroness O'Neill noted the paradox that we still depend on the very people who we claim not to trust. She argued that new mechanisms of accountability and targets undermine the professionals on whom the public sector depends, and create a culture of suspicion and low morale which may increase public distrust.

Ruth Fox, director of the Hansard Society's Parliament

and Government programme, wrote a fascinating report just before the general election entitled 'What's trust got to do with it? – Public Trust in and Expectations of Politicians and Parliament', on the basis of a working group organised with the Political Studies Association and the Centre for Citizenship, Globalisation and Governance at the University of Southampton. She noted that levels of public trust in politicians as individuals have not collapsed recently, since they were already low. Indeed,

politicians, by focusing on policies designed to engender trust, have missed the bigger, broader underlying concern. They cannot readily regain what they have never really possessed, namely trust, but they have lost satisfaction, relevance and influence in recent decades, and perhaps by focusing reforms so much on trust, they have helped to exacerbate this loss themselves.

What is needed is a sense both of the relevance of politicians and political institutions, and a closer engagement by them with voters.

CHAPTER NINE

WHAT CAN BE DONE

Politicians will never be loved, respected or trusted. But we cannot do without them – even if we can do without many of the current lot. If we get rid of many MPs – as happened at the 2010 general election – we are merely replacing them with another lot of members largely in the same mould. The question is, rather, whether we can do anything to make politics work better – for them and for us, the voters. In this final chapter, I put forward some recommendations, highlighted in bold, about how they can improve their standing. These specific proposals are distinct from general observations about how politicians, and the media, might do politics differently.

The Conservative–Liberal Democrat coalition has proposed several measures of political reform. Some, as discussed below, may help, but others are largely irrelevant to the position of politicians. The populist mantra of cutting the cost of politics has produced two well-publicised proposals which are likely to be counter-productive. First, the pre-election commitment to reducing the number of politically appointed special advisers below the pre-election level of seventy-eight – to an initial total of sixty-eight – was a symbolic gesture at best since the savings were likely to be minimal. But the proposal turned out to be perverse in the context of the coalition, where experience from both Scotland and Wales has shown that you need more, not fewer, special advisers. This is to ensure that the two parties work closely together – particularly since there are five departments with no Lib Dem ministers. The insistence that this pledge cannot be broken means that people are being appointed as temporary civil servants, on short-term contracts, to fulfil the type of role which a special adviser would normally do. So important rules aimed at preserving the impartiality of civil servants are being bent so that ministers can still claim, misleadingly, that they are cutting the number of special advisers, and the cost of politics – when, in practice, there are no real savings.

Second, the number of MPs will be reduced from 650 to 600 after the next general election. But this will probably produce only very small savings since the amount of constituency work will not be cut but will be redistributed among fewer MPs. The consequent review of constituency boundaries, and the new rules aimed at producing constituencies nearer in numbers of voters to each other, will result in changes in the majority of seats.

Consequently, sitting MPs will spend much of the next few years competing against each other for party nominations. This will be a distraction from the main work of MPs. Far more important than cutting the number of MPs is reducing the size of the payroll vote – ministers and parliamentary private secretaries – which has grown steadily over the past two decades and increases the executive's influence within the legislature.

Recommendation 1:
The existing statutory limits on numbers of paid ministers in the Commons should be enforced to prevent Prime Ministers appointing additional unpaid ministers (those only receiving a backbench MP's pay) and the number of PPSs could be limited to one per department. In the longer term the maximum number of permitted ministers should be reduced in line with the cut in the size of the Commons, as recommended by the Public Administration Committee of the Commons.

The coalition's two other key proposals have been the referendum on whether to shift to the Alternative Vote and creating a fixed five-year term for parliaments. The impact of each change would probably be much less than either its supporters or critics claim. AV is not a proportional system and its effect on party strengths depends on how well the third party is doing, and whether voters' behaviour changes. Whether or not a parliament lasts a full five years is largely a matter of political will and the ability of the government to retain a Commons majority. If hung parliaments, and hence coalitions, become more frequent, there is a case for allowing a change of the governing combination without automatically triggering a general election, as would usually happen if a government lost a vote of confidence. But if there is to be a statutory maximum term, it should be four, not five, years. Overall, such changes are likely to have a limited impact on the public's view of politicians.

What should happen at Westminster
MPs, and peers, need to address three areas: first, their own conduct; second, their own effectiveness; and, third, their connection with the public. First, politicians – both MPs and

peers – will remain the subject of media scrutiny and popular, and populist, scorn until they have sorted out their financial affairs. This is not just about cleaning up the past mess, which is gradually happening as past miscreants are either subject to the internal disciplinary mechanisms of both Houses or dealt with by the courts, and, in some cases, imprisoned. Both Houses have put in place new systems for expenses/allowances which should reduce the scope for abuse. However, the squabbling over the work of IPSA is both distracting MPs and continuing to undermine public confidence in Parliament. Some of the complaints over the application of the new expenses regime are justified: the bureaucratic nature of the claims system and its complexity, the arbitrary nature of the definition of the London area for travelling and hence qualification for accommodation expenses for living away from home, and the impact on family life.

The key principles are that MPs should not determine their own allowances and that they should be paid and monitored independently. But MPs need expenses – not as a personal benefit to boost their pay as the tabloids often, wrongly allege – but to meet the costs of running a constituency office, to travel between their constituency and Westminster, and to employ and equip staff. The main problems identified in IPSA's review in March 2011 are being addressed.

But provided that the system of claiming is made simpler, MPs are doing their cause no good by continuing to complain. They know there is scant sympathy for them, either in the media or the public. Moreover, if the controversy over IPSA dies down, MPs can be less defensive about their quite legitimate expenses and their still pretty modest salaries (£65,738 at the time of writing). There is a good deal of hypocrisy in media comment about MPs on the make and take written by journalists, especially the more populist columnists, earning more than this.

The recent imprisonment of some MPs over their expenses shows that serious abuse does not escape punishment. All parties have promised to introduce procedures for recalling MPs found guilty by the Commons of serious ethical misconduct, short of the automatic disqualification for any MP given a sentence of twelve months or more. This would allow voters to force a by-election, and is aimed at MPs such as Derek Conway who remained in the Commons for over two years despite being censured and suspended over abuse of his office expenses. Suspension is anyway a messy sanction since it deprives constituents of an MP working on their behalf. However, there are a number of traps: what type of offences would qualify? There is, at present, a blurred line between allegations of misconduct seen as disciplinary offences to be dealt with in either House, and criminal offences punishable by the courts. It is not always clear why an MP or peer has fallen one side of the line rather than the other. Who would decide that misconduct was sufficiently serious to justify triggering the recall mechanism? Should decisions be left just to MPs or should outsiders be involved? How much local support would be necessary to force a by-election? Would there be campaign spending limits on such a recall ballot? And how do you protect against campaigns by single-issue pressure groups calling for a recall of MPs who have taken unpopular stands on policy? This shows some of the problems of introducing an apparently simple solution to an exceptional problem.

Recommendation 2:
Any MP sentenced to a prison term of any length should be automatically disqualified from being a member, forcing a by-election, while any MP found guilty of gross ethical misconduct (by a panel including lay members as well as MPs, though subject to a vote of the full Commons) would automatically lose their seat, though be able to stand in the subsequent by-election.

Second, effectiveness. Despite increased knowledge about Parliament, the latest Hansard Audit shows that fewer people, 27 per cent, are now satisfied with it than at any time previously, the previous low being 33 per cent at the end of 2009. Just 30 per cent now agree that Parliament is 'working for you and me', down from 38 per cent a year earlier. One of the hardest tasks of politicians is to demonstrate what they achieve. There are, of course, two aspects. The predominant one in peoples' minds is how the government of the day is performing, and the latest figures reflect increased worries about the impact of public spending cuts and worries over prospects for living standards and jobs. Public attitudes to politics and politicians have, in the past, been strongly influenced by their view of current performance rather than structures of governance. Understandably, perhaps, there is interest in the second aspect, the success or otherwise of MPs and peers in holding the government to account. This is hardly surprising since what happens in Parliament gets so little coverage.

As I argued in Chapter Five, the Commons and Lords are both less supine and more effective than is commonly asserted. The development of the select committee system has substantially strengthened the scrutiny role of the Commons, and the creation of the Backbench Business Committee after the 2010 general election has given ordinary MPs more of a say over the choice of at least some debates. There is a lot more that could, and should, be done. Whenever I say or write that, there is always the whisper in my ear from a long-serving clerk of the Commons warning against adding even more committees or more work to already stretched MPs. The risk is always that suggesting more duties for select committees will produce patchy results since MPs will not be able to do more work. There are twin dangers: one is of trying to run Parliament into the government. The job of MPs is to scrutinise, not, unless they are ministers, to govern; the second, a common error of outside critics, is to regard Parliament as a distinct institution separate from the executive. We do not have separation of powers and therefore there will always be an ambiguity over the role of MPs, facing several roles and loyalties, to their constituents, to their party and to their role as members of the Commons.

With all these caveats, MPs could demonstrate and strengthen their effectiveness by:

Recommendation 3:
Agreeing minimum standards of clarity in drafting Bills before they can be introduced; require pre-legislative scrutiny to examine the implementation and workability of Bills by departmental select committees, and occasionally joint committees of both Houses, as the norm (with inevitable, very limited exceptions just after a general election); restore a collaborative approach to the timetabling of Bills both in committee and report stages (as part of the promised introduction of a House Business Committee to determine the whole Commons agenda); and making a greater commitment to using new procedures for post-legislative scrutiny.

The overall aim of these proposals (which have been made by, among others, the Hansard Society and the Better Government Initiative) is to provide time and flexibility for the flaws in legislation to be revealed during parliamentary debates and then to be remedied, producing better quality legislation which does not then need to be amended. This is one of the main complaints of outside bodies, from lawyers and accountants to businesses, charities and voters.

Recommendation 4:
The strengthening of the independence of select committees by the election of their chairs and members is just a first step. It should be made easier for committees to summon both 'people and papers' since their theoretical powers, involving going to the full chamber, are virtually never used. The role of committees in approving public appointments needs to be reviewed with a sliding scale of power, depending on the importance of the appointment, from blocking a nomination and forcing ministers to think again, down to merely offering a non-binding comment (as suggested by the Institute for Government, 2011). Committees also need to think more about their strategies for scrutiny rather than following an ad hoc approach. The experiment in December 2010 of allowing a committee chair to make a short statement, and be questioned by MPs, on a new report on the floor of the Commons should be expanded. In return, MPs – particularly ambitious new ones – need to show their own commitment, both by turning up in larger numbers to committee sessions and not leaving within a few months when offered a shadow frontbench post or to become a parliamentary private secretary. There ought to be an informal understanding among the party leaders that

they do not offer any new MP such a post during the first session after a general election.

The House of Lords often prides itself on its superiority to the Commons, in standards of conduct, in performing its scrutiny role over legislation and in its select committees. The predominantly appointed House is unquestionably more active, better-attended and more assiduous than in the past. But it is not as good as many peers like to claim – and its problems have been exacerbated by the big influx of new peers, and a more partisan tone created by the change in balance of parties following the formation of the coalition. Peers like to proclaim the virtues of their self-regulatory system but they often seem to equate that with no regulation – a dilemma which has been examined by a leaders' group under Lord Goodlad. Lords question time frequently descends into winner-take-all noisy exchanges in which the assertive dominate questions. Similarly, ministerial statements can be turgid affairs in which opposition spokesmen and peers give verbose responses rather than pose questions.

The Lords always points to its role in improving legislation, but that is largely by comparison with the often hurried working of the Commons. The procedures of the Lords can be streamlined, both through more pre-legislative scrutiny, co-ordinated with the Commons, and by holding more committee sessions outside the main chamber. The Lords select committee system has many virtues, notably the deployment of non-partisan experts and in the depth of its work. But its coverage is patchy. There is no committee responsible for public services, despite the presence in the House of distinguished people from the medical and legal professions, from the police (let alone the lawyers), from social services and education.

Recommendation 5:

There is a strong case for the Lord Speaker to be given the power at least to pick questioners, as Mr Speaker does in the Commons, alternating between various groups. The current Lords review of working practices should lead to a less insular approach, and a greater willingness to co-ordinate legislative and scrutiny work with the Commons (which need not compromise the independence of the Lords), with a wider range of select committees.

Longer-term reform of the Lords is now returning to the centre of the political debate, to the apprehension and excitement of peers. With the publication of the government's draft Bill, there will now be a lengthy process of pre-legislative scrutiny. The key principles should be that the Lords should be different in its powers (revising and non-financial), different in its method of selection, and different in its membership. The value of the current House lies in these differences. Nothing would be worse than a change which produced a chamber similar to the Commons in its membership being overwhelmingly career politicians. Not only would this produce conflict between the two Houses vying over which is the most legitimate, but it would also remove the many talented and experienced people who now serve as peers. That is why I am unconvinced about a wholly elected House and would favour keeping a minimum of 20 per cent appointed crossbench peers. Such a group would provide a balance and prevent even a coalition of two parties having a certain majority – as has been shown since May 2010 when even the Conservatives and Liberal Democrats combined have from time to time been defeated by Labour and the crossbenchers.

The creation of the coalition – and the big influx of new

peers – have already changed the mood of the House, as was shown in the occasional filibustering by Labour peers, and the use of the supposedly exceptional procedure of closure motions to curtail debate twice, during the passage of the Parliamentary Voting System and Constituencies Act. This raised questions over the conventions governing relations between the two Houses, notably the Salisbury–Addison agreement in the late 1940s that the Lords does not vote against the second reading of Bills which have appeared in the governing parties' manifesto nor pass wrecking amendments. But the coalition agreement has superseded the two parties' manifestos. While peers retreated from the brink over the voting and boundaries act, there is a case for a review of the conventions – ahead of any longer term changes in composition of the Lords.

Recommendation 6:
A reformed House of Lords should be different in composition and method of selection than the Commons with at least a fifth of crossbench members appointed to provide expertise and independence. The existing conventions on relations between the Houses need to be reviewed both to reaffirm the primacy of the Commons and to preserve the independent scrutiny and revising role of the Lords. This might involve a package whereby the Lords has a set period before a Bill is returned to the Commons (say, sixty parliamentary days, as suggested by the 1968 White Paper on Lords reform and by a Labour peers' group in 2004), while self-regulation is underpinned by the creation of a Business Committee, consisting of all groups, including crossbenchers and backbench peers.

None of these six recommendations is going to excite voters

or the media. But together they will make Parliament more effective in doing its core job of holding ministers to account and helping to improve the quality of legislation. Their public impact will depend crucially on the third key issue for MPs: their connection with voters. For many, Parliament appears a remote institution with little relevance to their everyday lives. That is partly a matter of the language and rituals which take considerable time to explain to newcomers to Westminster. In that sense, the over-used village comparison is right. It is easy enough – as I know from my days as a journalist – to become absorbed in the seductive world of Parliament. But MPs and peers should always be thinking about how their actions appear to outsiders. Too often, their instinctive reaction is to close ranks. At least, MPs have been forced to recognise their unpopularity by their constituents. But peers have no constituents and too many just talk among themselves, reinforcing a sense of injured self-righteousness.

Engagement can take many forms. At one level, there is political education, where the current Mr Speaker and Lord Speaker have been innovators on outreach, both personally and in encouraging MPs and peers, to go out, especially in schools, to explain what happens at Westminster. The Information and Education departments of both Houses have developed a series of excellent schemes to inform and involve young people, while the parliamentary website allows many more people to understand what is happening day to day and hour to hour. In this respect, it would be a retrograde step if citizenship education was removed from the national curriculum since this provides one of the ways in which many youngsters have the chance to learn about how our democracy operates. Most MPs already run active and informative websites. These should be the norm, and constituents should be entitled to expect a specified level of service in this way. The Hansard Society has worked with the Lords in creating and supporting Lords of the Blog, an entertaining and informative site about what happens in the Lords, But too few peers participate. Peers do not have individual constituents but they do have a broader responsibility to the public. Why should not every peer have a website where he or she explains what they do and invite comments?

Parliament should engage more directly with voters on issues of the day. Many MPs individually do participate in online debates and consultations with voters. The House of Lords collaborated with the BBC's 'Have Your Say' and Democracy Live websites, and through Parliament's Facebook page, to get people's views on the value of good parenting in preparing children for school ahead of a debate in February 2011. A summary of these comments was forwarded to peers who had put their names down to speak, while Lord Northbourne, who initiated the debate, took part in a live web chat. During and after the debate people could continue to respond to the discussion. This approach could, and should, be applied more generally. The coalition agreement suggested that the Commons should introduce a new public reading stage for Bills to give the public an opportunity to comment on proposed legislation online for use in a dedicated 'public reading day' within a Bill's committee stage. Care would have to be taken that ordinary voters have the chance to comment, as well as familiar pressure and interest groups. As a pilot, the public has been given a chance to comment on line on the Protection of Freedom Bill, intended to cut back the state's interventions in peoples' lives.

Recommendation 7:
Voters should be entitled to a minimum standard of service from MPs – a specified length of time to answer constituents' emails and letters and to provide substantive answers. Monitoring and redressing mechanisms would be tricky, but the mere publication of such standards would provide a benchmark for voters to hold their constituency representative to account. All MPs should provide websites where constituents can discuss issues with other constituents.

Petitions and direct democracy

The coalition government has made several proposals to involve voters more directly in political decisions. For instance, any petition that secures 100,000 signatures within a given year would be eligible for formal debate in Parliament, and that petition with the most signatures would be tabled as a Bill. Many MPs are very wary of these ideas for fear of unleashing populist campaigns backed by tabloid papers on highly emotive issues such as bringing back capital punishment, stopping further immigration, slashing welfare benefits or withdrawing from the European Union. The suggested petitions would only be agenda-setting since decisions on whether to take petitions or a Bill further would be determined by the votes of MPs. I favour the increased use of petitions to allow voters to raise issues which must then be considered by MPs. The trouble with the 10 Downing Street petitions site, which was launched in the dying days of the Blair government, was that it was, in effect, a one-way process. No matter how many signatures, all petitioners got was a statement from the relevant minister, generally a bland repetition of existing policy. There was no opportunity for the petition to be considered and debated. That just invites cynicism and public disillusionment.

The attraction of the new proposal is that only well-supported petitions will be considered. The aim is to demonstrate that Parliament is not out of touch with voters. The risk, however, is that expectations will be raised by campaigns to get signatures for popular petitions which will then be dashed when MPs vote against a proposal – as they would do, say, on any call to restore capital punishment (as they have in every such vote for nearly half a century). So there would be a clash between the voice of the People and what would undoubtedly be portrayed as an out of touch elite. I do not regard that as an argument against petitions. MPs should directly address such populist calls, and seek to defeat them in argument, not evade them. The belief that politicians have been patronising, and misleading, voters on questions such as Europe and immigration is one of the reasons for public disenchantment with politicians, and why support for extremist parties has risen. A petitions system would force politicians to address such arguments.

Recommendation 8:
Public petitions should be introduced to trigger debates in the Commons, and, in very few cases, to introduce Bills, as proposed by the coalition agreement. In addition, they should also initiate scrutiny of issues by select committees. But these should be strictly agenda-setting, leading to debates and committee scrutiny, with decisions on how far to take proposals remaining with Parliament. This would reaffirm the essential principle of representative democracy.

The crucial exception is the use of the referendum, more

promised than occurring. The problem here is determining when they should be held. The contortions of the Blair and Brown governments over the EU constitution and then the Lisbon treaty show what a quagmire this is. The coalition government's EU legislation would require a referendum to be held if a substantial transfer of powers from Westminster to European institutions is proposed, but, as eurosceptics point out, that is full of ambiguities. What domestic constitutional changes should require a referendum? The Constitution Committee of the House of Lords, in a report on referendums in the UK shortly before the 2010 general election, was generally sceptical about their use and regretted their ad hoc use as a tactical device by the government of the day. Nonetheless, the committee accepted that referendums were most appropriately used for 'fundamental constitutional issues', such as proposals to abolish the monarchy, to leave the European Union, for any of the nations of the UK to leave the union, to abolish either House of Parliament, to change the electoral system for the House of Commons, to adopt a written constitution, and to change the UK's system of currency. A written or codified constitution could provide a more precise definition of such constitutional issues. However, that still leaves many uncertainties. Every new referendum is treated completely afresh, within the broad regulatory framework of the Electoral Commission. There is no agreement about whether referendums should be held before substantial legislation is put to Parliament (as in the case of Scottish and Welsh devolution and the London mayor), or afterwards (as in the case of changing the electoral system to AV). There are arguments about whether there should be a threshold level of support, in terms of turnout, which scuppered Scottish devolution in 1979, and was eventually rejected for the AV referendum.

Recommendation 9:
The government should initiate a debate in both Houses of Parliament to seek cross-support on the circumstances in which national referendums should be held. The principle should be that they should only be for 'fundamental constitutional issues' and they should be post-legislative (held after the substantive measure enacting the change has been approved).

I am sceptical, however, about calls for more direct democracy via citizens' juries and deliberative assemblies. As I argued earlier in the book, the risk is that these become self-selecting groups of already committed and active citizens, who are, by definition, unrepresentative. There is ample survey evidence that most people are neither active nor want to be – as opposed to having credit-card membership of a voluntary group or charity. The latest Hansard Audit showed that just 4 per cent claimed to have taken part in a demonstration, picket or march over the last two or three years, and just 6 per cent said they had been to a political meeting. Fewer than one in ten had been an officer in an organisation or club. Moreover, a clear majority say they would not even like to be involved in decision-making for the country as a whole. A mere 7 per cent say they will definitely or probably become involved in a political party over the next few years, a third of the number saying the same about spending time in a local neighbourhood or community group. The scope for greater direct or participatory democracy seems to be mainly at such a neighbourhood level.

The challenge for parties

Political parties are the weak link in the politicians' armour. They are necessary to provide cohesion for a representative system, and as a recruiting ground for new MPs and ministers. But the main parties now rest on a very narrow base of support – only about one in fifty of the electorate belong to a party. Yet, leaving aside the Scottish and Welsh nationalists, and the members for Northern Ireland, the three main parties provide virtually all MPs. Various attempts to boost membership have achieved at best only short-lived success as the electoral cycle moves in the party's favour. This long-term decline in membership partly reflects deeper social trends as well as a specific drop in identification with the main parties.

The weak membership bases of the parties raise two main questions: over their funding and over the candidates they put forward for elections. The increasing dependence of parties on big donations from wealthy individuals or bodies like the trade unions, rather than individual members or small contributions, tarnishes the reputation of politics, and politicians, and has been very damaging over the past two decades. If some of the donors are genuinely public spirited, as some undoubtedly are, there have been too many allegations of donations/ loans in return for knighthoods and peerages, and, even more importantly, access to political leaders, for comfort. There are no easy answers as the failed attempt by Sir Hayden Phillips to broker a package of reforms in the last parliament showed. The vested interests of the two big parties blocked any deal. We need healthy parties so any attempt to restrict the size of donations needs to be balanced by new incentives, and limited taxpayer support, to encourage parties to seek new members, supporters and contributions.

While voters are understandably hostile to their money going to parties, and politicians, there is already substantial state support via the 'Short' money for opposition parties in the Commons, and the parallel, though more limited, 'Cranborne' support in the Lords.

Recommendation 10:
Any party finance package should include a low cap on individual and institutional donations of no more than, say, £10,000 a year; a positive decision every four or five years to opt-in to the political levy by trade union members; and, to balance the resulting squeeze on the finances of the parties, some form of either tax relief, such as gift aid for small donations, or matching state support for any contribution up to £100 a year.

As worrying is that the narrow membership base of parties also limits the choice of candidates for office. Politics is becoming increasingly professionalised, with those seeking to enter the Commons taking jobs as special advisers, party researchers, lobbyists and the like in their twenties after leaving university and seldom pursuing an independent career outside politics. Just look at the current leaders of the main parties, David Cameron, Nick Clegg and Ed Miliband – or other leading figures like Ed Balls or George Osborne. Virtually all their adult lives have been spent in, or very near, party politics. They represent the political class, whom Peter Oborne corruscatingly dismissed in his 2007 book *The Triumph of the Political Class* that I mentioned in Chapter One. When I wrote my own book warning about these trends in 1993 – *Honest Opportunism: the rise of the career politician* – I had the disconcerting experience after the 1997 election of some new

MPs from both main parties coming up to me saying how useful they had found it as a guide to their advancement – not quite what I intended.

The rise of the career politician has contradictory effects. On the one hand, it underlines the sense of politicians being cut off from the public. But, on the other hand, their apprenticeships as special advisers and staffers does prepare potential MPs for the political life much better than those who come in with little or no previous political experience. It certainly helps a potential minister to have experience of working in a large organisation before becoming a minister since most MPs are sole or small traders with their tiny parliamentary staffs. However, few businessmen have been successful at the Cabinet level in politics, though some have made an impact at a medium level in handling less partisan areas of policy like trade or science.

There would be undoubted gains from recruiting a wider range of people to become MPs – even if the glittering prizes are always likely to go to the already committed, career politicians. After the expenses scandal, the Conservative Party, in particular, made a big effort to recruit people who had never been politically involved by opening up the candidates' list in a desire to 'clean up' politics, As Byron Criddle points out (in *The British General* Election edited by Dennis Kavanagh and Philip Cowley, 2010), some 4,000 people responded, of whom about 400 were put through the candidate screening process, with 200 passing. Eventually four were selected, a soldier, a doctor, a former traveller and diplomat, and a journalist (who happened to be the brother of Boris Johnson, the London Mayor). They 'may have been new to party politics, but in social and professional background and gender, they cut a very traditional dash'.

The Conservatives also held open primaries, allowing registered electors who were not party members to attend the final selection meeting – in the hope of recruiting new members and of opening out the party. Only fifteen of the 116 seats where open primaries were Conservative held, although forty-eight of these seats were gained by the party at the election. Criddle writes that 'the possibilities of entryism – the swamping of the meeting by outsiders – was slight, with the non-party members usually comprising no more than a minority of those attending the open primaries'. In two constituencies, there were all-postal ballots where the entire electorate was offered a postal vote to choose the Conservative candidate. This was on the basis of short-lists chosen by the local parties. In Totnes, where the turnout was 25 per cent, the least political of the three candidates – Sarah Wollaston, a nearby doctor who had been in the Conservative Party for only two years – was picked. She has proved to be a notably independent-minded MP, especially on health issues. In Gosport, where the turnout was 18 per cent, the winner was also a woman, Caroline Dinenage, but a more political figure who had fought a nearby seat. There is no evidence, however, that this boosted turnout above the local average in either seat. The Tories did, however, succeed in raising their total of women MPs from seventeen to forty-nine, by a combination of exhortation and skewing the pool of candidates in favour of women and ethnic minorities (where the number of MPs rose from two to eleven). Despite these advances, Labour still had more in both groups.

Nonetheless, the 2010 general election also saw a further rise in the numbers of professional politicians, notably on the Labour side where a fifth of MPs, and two-fifths of the new intake, were previously employed as ministerial or MPs' aides.

As I argued above, many of these turn out to be good MPs. However, all parties might follow the Conservative example and consider either variant of open primary. The coalition agreement opened the possibility of state support for such primaries, though this idea has been shelved for the time being on cost grounds. The traditional objection, especially from the trade unions on the Labour side, that this would allow in outsiders without a commitment to a party misses the point. The parties have such small membership that they need to encourage participation by outsiders to ensure democratic legitimacy for their candidates.

Recommendation 11:
All parties need to broaden the range of candidates they select and the number of people involved in selection. As they are voluntary bodies, the method should be up to them – though matching taxpayer funding or tax relief could be made dependent on opening up selection processes. But the parties should be encouraged – possibly via free postage – to undertake more Totnes and Gosport style primaries.

How governments can defend politics – and politicians
Governments – both current and potential – also have a responsibility beyond that of MPs and parties. They need to be honest about what politics involves. Of course, political leaders need to offer a vision and objectives. But they should not raise false, and unrealisable, expectations of what can be achieved in practice. Democratic politics is generally about incremental steps – often quite big ones, but seldom revolutionary ones. It is about reaching compromises between conflicting interests. That is desirable. Experiments, pilots,

pathfinders or whatever you like to call them, are preferable to wholesale transformations, as the present coalition government may discover as it seeks across-the-board changes to all public services at the same time.

Ministers, and shadow spokesmen, should be more modest in their aspirations and claims. Oppositions would be wise not to attack, and promise to repeal, everything an incumbent government does. Such instant changes are often themselves reversed before long, damaging both the services affected and the reputation of politicians. This is not to argue for a soggy bipartisan centrism: far from it. But governments would generally do better to recognise that policies evolve and should aim to adjust rather than tear up and start again.

Similarly, both governments and oppositions need to recognise the complexity of taking and implementing decisions. That involves risks and things going wrong. Of course, errors should be recognised and corrected. But politicians would gain from not over-claiming or over-criticising. Gordon Brown did himself no good by his assertions in his Budget speeches that he had banished 'boom and bust' and that he was presiding over the longest period of sustained growth for 100, 200 or even 300 years, the period lengthened every year (no matter that there were no reliable national income statistics until the 1940s). So when the boom went bust from 2008 onwards, Brown was punished for hubris, even though the main cause of the downturn was the international banking crisis. The lesson is clear. It is always best to be open with voters.

National politicians would also benefit from genuinely decentralising decisions to a local level, and local politicians, where possible. This would mean that ministers in London would have to take responsibility, and the blame, for activities which should properly be run in cities, towns and counties. Normally, talk of localism is humbug, and it will only mean something when local authorities are made responsible for raising a higher proportion of their budgets. This would link council tax – and any other taxes they might raise or introduce – to what they spend. This is, in a sense, the definition of representative democracy.

Ministers should also not be ashamed of being politicians. They should be more robust, especially in their dealings with the media. They often sound too defensive: too eager to depoliticise issues which are inherently political. It makes sense to create arm's-length bodies to administer some functions of government and to allow some regulatory bodies to be independent of day-to-day political interference. But decisions on levels of spending and taxation, and on the allocation of resources can, and should, only be taken by politicians who are accountable to voters.

Recommendation 12:
Making politicians more responsible for their actions needs to be extended to the local level, with increased freedom for devolved bodies and local authorities to raise taxes and to introduce new ones. This should be linked to the spread of directly elected mayors to every city and sizeable town, to strengthen local leadership and to provide a visible link with voters.

The media – the feral beast tamed
The media should be questioning, irreverent and robust – as they always have been in Britain. Politicians should not expect a quiet life from newspapers, broadcasters, and, now,

the internet. But that does not mean the snide, cynical and destructive coverage that is too often the norm nowadays. There is, as I have argued throughout this book, a distinction between particular politicians, whose foibles and errors should be exposed, and politicians as a class who are central to the existence of representative democracy. At present, the two groups are confused and the whole tenor of the coverage is negative about politics as an activity. MPs are depicted as on the take/gravy train when they earn a salary which is lower than many journalists and when they claim expenses which are purely to pay for necessary staff. Any detail of their private lives is regarded as fair game for press intrusion, however irrelevant it may be for the performance of their public duties.

Above all, the media need to allow space for politicians to reach the compromises and deals that are central to any successful representative democracy. Instead of complaining about U-turns and betrayal, the media should recognise such manoeuvres and concessions as the only way to govern on behalf of a country that consists of a large number of different interests and opinions. Instead of protesting that every difference of opinion is a deep split, every personal mishap is the worst scandal ever, and that all civil servants are idle pen-pushers (slightly odd in the era of the keyboard) and that all politicians are arrogant, out of touch and probably corrupt, the media should recognise that politics, like most of life, is painted in grey, rather than in vivid primary colours.

This sounds utopian and it cannot, of course, be mandated. But a reminder of what a reasonable, and robust, dialogue would look like would give a benchmark to readers and viewers.

Talk of reforming the media is pointless, if not harmful, since codes or concordats are usually full of pious platitudes.

The current Press Complaints Commission is inadequate and needs strengthening to protect privacy and to be a more vigorous regulator, and punisher, of abuses. While readers and viewers should have a stronger, and, above all quicker, right of redress than now, statutory regulation would probably be counter-productive by inhibiting free speech and, in practice, favouring the powerful and the wealthy. I remain sceptical about suggestions that non-BBC outlets should be able to ditch impartiality. Despite increased diversity, the main broadcasters are still so influential that they should be legally required to maintain a broad balance. I do not want to see *Sky News* – which rightly enjoys a high reputation, though very different from the BBC or ITN – from going down the route of Fox News in the USA. Rather, I see hope in the internet which widens the opportunity for both news and comment. It can and is being abused by the strident and the excessively partisan. But the internet also offers the chance for a wider range of media organisations, as well as individuals, to report and express their opinions. It allows many, many more of us directly to see, and hear, what is being said in Parliament than ever read newspaper reports of Commons speeches. Politicians now also have the chance to communicate directly with voters.

Tony Wright summed the debate up rather neatly in his lecture, in early 2009, just before the full expenses scandal erupted. He argued that we should do politics differently:

What might this mean? Well, politicians could play it straight. Journalists could play it fair. Parties could resist the rise of a political class. Ministers could make sure that Cabinet government works. MPs could decide that Parliament matters (and clean up their expenses!).

Interest groups could say who should have less if they are to have more. Civil servants should tell truth to power. Governments could promise less and perform more. Could start writing in good plain English. The blogosphere could exchange rant for reason. Electors could decide to become critical citizens.

Amen to all the above. We voters also need to learn to expect less and to complain less. But politicians also have it in their power to do more than grumble about being misunderstood and unloved.

They can be more positive and assertive about what they do. They can take actions – in line with the twelve recommendations made in this chapter – which would show they are in touch with voters and are acting on their behalf. That might even strengthen the case for their defence.

BIBLIOGRAPHY

Allen, Nicholas, and Birch, Sarah, 'Political Conduct and Misconduct: Probing Public Opinion', *Parliamentary Affairs* (2011), vol. 64, no. 1

Barber, Lionel, 'Hugh Cudlipp lecture', London, 31 January 2010

Bingham, Tom, *The Rule of Law* (London: Allen Lane, 2010)

Blair, Tony, Reuters speech on the media, June 2007, reprinted with commentaries in *Political Quarterly* (2007), vol. 78, no. 4

Blair, Tony, *A Journey* (London: Hutchinson, 2010)

Bogdanor, Vernon, *The New British Constitution* (Oxford and Portland, Oregon: 2009)

National Centre for Social Research, *British Social Attitudes Survey, 27th Report*, London, 2010

Brooke, Heather, *The Silent State: Secrets, Surveillance and the Myth of British Democracy* (London: Heinemann, 2010)

Cameron, David, speech on the Big Society, Liverpool, 19 July 2010

Campbell, Alastair, *The Blair Years* (London: Hutchinson, 2007)

Campbell, Alastair, *Diaries (uncut): Volume One: Prelude to Power 1994-97* (London: Hutchinson, 2010)

Campbell, Alastair, *Diaries (uncut): Volume Two: Power and the People, 1997-99* (London: Hutchinson, 2011)

Cowley, Philip, *The Rebels, How Blair mislaid his majority* (London: Politico's, 2005)

Cowley, Philip, and Stuart, Mark, www.revolts.co.uk

Crick, Bernard, *In Defence of Politics,* 4th edn (London: Penguin Press, 1992)

Flinders, Matthew, 'In Defence of Politics', inaugural lecture, University of Sheffield, May 2010, in *Political Quarterly* (2010), vol. 81, no. 3

Foster, Christopher, *British Government in Crisis, or The Third English Revolution* (Oxford: Hart Publishing, 2005)

Fox, Ruth, *What's Trust got to do with it? Public Trust in and Expectations of Politicians and Parliament* (London, Hansard Society; Political Studies Association; the Centre for Citizenship, Globalisation and Governance, 2010)

Fox, Ruth, and Korris, Matt, *Making Better Law: Reform of the legislative process from policy to Act* (London: Hansard Society, 2010)

Giddings, Philip, (*ed.*) *The Future of Parliament: Issues for a New Century* (London: Palgrave Macmillan, 2005)

Hansard Society, *The Challenge for Parliament – Making Government Accountable* (London: Hansard Society, 2001)

Hansard Society, Audit of Political Engagement, annually 2004 to 2011

Hay, Colin, *Why We Hate Politics* (Cambridge: Polity Press, 2007)

HC Liaison Committee 1st Report, *Shifting the Balance: Select Committees and the Executive* (HL Paper (1999–2000) no.

300)

HC Public Administration Committee 5th Report, *Smaller Government: Shrinking the Quango State* (HC Paper (2010-11) no. 537)

HC Reform Committee (The Wright Committee) 1st Report *Rebuilding the House* (HC Paper (2008-09) no. 1117)

HL Constitution Committee 12th Report *Referendums in the United Kingdom* (HL Paper (2009-10) no. 99)

Institute for Government (Tom Gash, Ian Magee, Jill Rutter, Nicole Smith), *Read Before Burning: How to increase the effectiveness and accountability of quangos* (London, 2010)

Institute for Government, (Akash Paun and David Atkinson), *Balancing Act: The Right Role for Parliament in Public Appointments* (London, 2011)

Kavanagh, Dennis, and Cowley, Philip, *The British General Election of 2010* (London: Palgrave Macmillan, 2010)

Kelly, Sir Christopher, 'Trust, Transparency and Care', speech to the LSE Annual Health and Social Care Lecture, 17 May 2010

King, Anthony, *The British Constitution* (Oxford: Oxford University Press, 2007)

Laws, David, *22 Days In May: The Birth of the Lib Dem–Conservative Coalition* (London: Biteback, 2010)

Lloyd, John, *What the Media are Doing to Our Politics* (London: Constable, 2004)

Lloyd, John, 'Power Struggle', Life and Arts section of the *Financial Times*, January 8/9, 2011

Mancuso, Maureen, 'Ethical Attitudes of British MPs', *Parliamentary Affairs* (1993), vol. 46, no. 2

Marquand, David, *Decline of the Public: The Hollowing out of Citizenship* (Cambridge: Polity Press, 2004)

Maude, Francis, 'Bigger the Better', *New Statesman*, 4 October, 2010

McHugh, Declan, 'Wanting to be Heard But Not Wanting to Act? Addressing Political Disengagement', *Political Quarterly* (2006), vol. 59, no. 3

Norton, Philip, speech in House of Lords debate on Democracy: Power Inquiry, Thursday 15 June 2006

Oborne, Peter, *The Triumph of the Political Class* (London: Simon and Schuster, 2007)

O'Neill, Onora, *Reith Lectures* (2002) London, BBC Radio 4, www.bbc.co.uk/radio4/reith2002/lectures

Power Report, *Power to the People: An Independent Inquiry into Britain's Democracy* (2006), The centenary project of the Joseph Rowntree Charitable Trust and the Joseph Rowntree Reform Trust

Price, Lance, *Where Power Lies, Prime Ministers v The Media* (London: Simon and Schuster, 2010)

Riddell, Peter, *The Thatcher Government* (Oxford: Martin Robertson, 1983)

—— *The Thatcher Era, and its Legacy* (Oxford: Basil Blackwell, 1991)

—— *Honest Opportunism – The Rise of the Career Politician* (London: Hamish Hamilton, 1993)

—— *Parliament under Pressure* (London: Victor Gollancz, 1998)

—— 'The Rise of the Ranters: Saving Political Journalism', in John Lloyd and Jean Seaton (*Eds.*), *What Can Be Done? Making the Media and Politics Better*, in association with *Political Quarterly* (Blackwell Publishing, 2006)

—— *The Unfulfilled Prime Minister, Tony Blair's quest for a legacy* (London: Politico's, 2005, *rev.* 2006)

—— 'In Defence of Politicians: In Spite of Themselves', *Parliamentary Affairs* (2010), vol. 63, no. 3

Robertson, John and McLaughlin, Elizabeth, 'The Quality of Discussion on the Economy in UK Political Blogs in 2008', *Parliamentary Affairs* (2011), vol. 64, no. 1

Russell, Meg, and Sciaria, Maria, *The House of Lords in 2005: A More Representative and Assertive Chamber?* (London: The Constitution Unit of Public Policy, 2006)

Stoker, Gerry, *Why Politics Matters, Making Democracy Work* (London: Palgrave Macmillan, 2006)

Trollope, Anthony, *The Warden*, The Barchester Chronicles (Oxford: Oxford University Press, 1982)

Willetts, David, *The Pinch: How the baby boomers took their children's future – and why they should give it back* (London: Atlantic Books, 2010)

Wright, Tony, 'Doing Politics Differently', *Political Quarterly* (2009), vol. 80, no. 3

Wright, Tony, 'What are MPs for?' *Political Quarterly* (2010), vol. 81, no. 3

Zernike, Kate, *Boiling Mad: Inside Tea Party America* (New York: Times Books, 2010)